An Election for the Ages

An Election for the Ages

Rossi vs. **Gregoire,** 2004

TROVA HEFFERNAN

Foreword by Secretary of State Sam Reed

WSU PRESS

Washington State University Press
Pullman, Washington

WASHINGTON STATE UNIVERSITY

Washington State University Press
PO Box 645910
Pullman, Washington 99164-5910
Phone: 800-354-7360
Fax: 509-335-8568
Email: wsupress@wsu.edu
Website: wsupress.wsu.edu

First printing 2010

Library of Congress Cataloging-in-Publication Data

Heffernan, Trova.
An election for the ages : Rossi vs. Gregoire, 2004 / Trova Heffernan; foreword by Secretary of State Sam Reed.
p. cm.
ISBN 978-0-87422-304-0 (alk. paper)
1. Governors—Washington (State)—Election—History—21st century. 2. Rossi, Dino. 3. Gregoire, Christine O. 4. Elections—Washington (State)—History—21st century. 5. Washington (State)—Politics and government—1951- I. Title.
JK9290.H44 2010
324.9797'044—dc22

2010013492

WSU PRESS
Fine Quality Books from the Pacific Northwest

Contents

Foreword

The 2004 race for Washington Governor will go down in history as one of the closest and most controversial of all time. The stunning turn of events that unfolded from April 1, 2004, to June 6, 2005, will consume researchers and future decision makers for years. Elections like 2004 are not easily forgotten.

A nearly flawless campaign for governor that allowed an underdog to catch the frontrunner, a fierce rivalry between political parties, and an embattled Secretary of State made news around the world and contributed to a political drama unmatched by any election in modern State history. And the race for Governor is only part of the story.

This account is an inside look at how this Secretary of State and his key executive and election staff leaders handled a wildly unpopular Primary change, the largest General Election in State history, hundreds of probing press calls a week, free-wheeling blog writers and talk-radio hosts, thousands of angry voters, stressed-out election workers, aggressive political parties, frantic and suspicious gubernatorial campaign teams, and five contentious court cases—including two in the State Supreme Court.

By the time the courtroom cleared for the last time, one candidate had permanently assumed duties as Governor, while the opponent—who actually won the first two ballot counts—began a new life outside of politics.

As Secretary of State, I personally survived questions about my integrity and two efforts to have me recalled from office. My intent in reliving the trials of the 2004 election is to provide some understanding, for history's sake, of the dynamics involved in a heated political battle that reached beyond a particular race to democracy itself.

More than anything, the 2004 gubernatorial election demonstrated the importance of the voting process to the very people it served. As they should, citizens expect and depend on fair and accurate elections.

Sam Reed
Washington Secretary of State
Office of the Secretary of State

Acknowledgments

First and foremost, the Office of Secretary of State owes a debt of gratitude to Washington voters. Their vocal response to the controversial election resulted in some of the most important changes in recent elections history. Equally important is the leadership that followed within the elections community itself, as administrators embraced and implemented substantial reform.

A detailed account of the 2004 Governor's Election would never have transpired without the vision, direction, and determination of Secretary of State Sam Reed, Assistant Secretary of State Steve Excell, and Elections Director Nick Handy. Their guiding belief that citizens can benefit from the trials of 2004—and the solutions that followed—will serve our State for decades to come.

The foundation of this account was laid by longtime Deputy Elections Director John Pearson—a leader in the elections community and highly regarded for his exceptional knowledge and grasp of the subject. John's expertise put the election, the recounts, and the resulting court case in context.

The many contributors whose hard work and dedication should be recognized include Stephanie Horn for shouldering this assignment and providing invaluable assistance at every phase, Erika Aust and Tami Neilson for their copy editing and attention to detail, Kathy Campbell whose design work helped bring this election story to life, Joanie Deutsch who—in addition to contributing to the research, content, and copy editing—ran the agency's communication shop, photographer Patrick McDonald for capturing images of some of the most memorable moments that transpired during the historic election, as well as Tami Davis, Dave Ammons, Brian Zylstra, Alex Gamboa, Katie Blinn, and Shane Hamlin for their leadership, editing skills, and guidance.

Prologue

Chasing dreams of a Governorship, two viable and sophisticated candidates had decided to run for Washington's top statewide post in 2004. The election will long be remembered as a remarkable milestone in State history. For the first time, two recounts were conducted for a statewide office. Also for the first time, litigation followed the recounts, calling into question the integrity and accuracy of the entire voting process.

Never before had the occupancy of the most important office in State government been so disputed for so long. Not until June 2005 did Washington voters know for certain who would be the next Governor. This historic election turned out to be the ultimate political cliffhanger, and, percentage-wise, the closest governor's election in American history.

Out of 2.8 million votes cast, the final margin—after the initial count from election day, a machine recount, and then a manual recount—was a razor-thin 133 votes. At one time during the third (manual) count with 38 of the 39 counties reporting in, and with Washington voters frantically clicking their browsers for the final county (King County) to report, the candidates stood a breathtaking 8 votes apart. While closer elections have been held, the total number of ballots cast, the remarkable closeness of the race, the dramatic events that unfolded, and the magnitude of the office at issue came together in a perfect storm to create an Election for the Ages.

This account of the 2004 Governor's race is written from the perspective of the Office of Secretary of State. As with all reports of this nature, a degree of subjectivity is inevitable. A conscious effort to avoid partisanship, however, has been a foremost objective.

The 2004 election for Governor of Washington will long be remembered as a remarkable milestone in state history.

Chapter One

The Perfect Storm

Like voters across the country who held their breath waiting for the next President to be named in 2000, Washingtonians in 2004 were glued to television sets and the Internet to find out who finally would be declared Governor of Washington. Election coverage appeared in all forms of the media. Throughout Washington and the nation, the story swept across the front pages of newspapers, led news broadcasts, and provided Internet bloggers with more material to respond to than they could possibly dream up.

This extraordinary moment in Washington's history was actually months in the making. The state's political divide, a Primary Election system in flux, and another contentious U.S. Presidential race all played a role in creating a perfect storm, reaching its most turbulent point in the winter of 2004.

The margin of victory for Washington's Governor-elect in 2004 was a stunning forty-six-ten-thousandth of 1 percent. The unbelievable closeness between the state's top two gubernatorial candidates was due in large part to Washington's fragile political balance. In any given election, one-third of Washington voters may consider themselves Republican, one-third as Democrat, and one-third as Independent (voting for candidates from any major or minor political party depending on a candidate's credentials).

Washington's Capitol Building, often ground zero of the fight for the Governor's Office, served as home base to protests and perpetual media coverage. *Office of the Secretary of State*

In many ways, the Evergreen State provides a microcosm of America's politically divided landscape. The state's Democratic and Republican spheres of domination generally are divided by the majestic Cascade Range, between the rainy metropolitan areas of western Washington, and the vast, drier, agricultural lands of the state's eastern regions. The densely populated communities around Puget Sound tend toward being liberal, whereas conservative voters are more typical in the smaller towns across the state. Moderate voters predominate throughout the suburban crescent wrapping around Everett, Seattle, and Tacoma, as well as the Vancouver area. These voters tend to be fiscally conservative, while being socially and environmentally moderate.

However, voters frequently leap across the political divide. Republicans sometimes win traditionally liberal areas, while Democrats can carry the more conservative regions. As recently as 2002, the Washington State Legislature was divided 49–49 in the House of Representatives, and 25–24 in the Senate.

Although in recent years the state has voted slightly more Democratic, a relatively even political divide remains. The delicate balance makes for lively legislative sessions, passionate political campaigns, and neck-to-neck contests that can keep the most seasoned political analyst guessing. As much as anything, Washington's political divide set the stage for the perfect storm in 2004.

The Primary Election Backlash

The erratic path of changes in the State's Primary Election system also played a major role. The emotions that culminated in the November 2004 Governor's election actually began escalating earlier in August, a month or so before the Primary Election. Voters assumed they would be nominating candidates in Washington's traditional blanket Primary. Few would have suspected that Primary Election changes and mechanics would draw more angry remarks and head shaking than mudslinging between rival campaigns. But in 2004, changes in Washington's Primary system did just that.

The controversy centered on voter freedom—pitting the electorate against political parties, and Washington Secretary of State Sam Reed, a longtime Republican, against insiders of his own party. As 2004 would demonstrate, Washingtonians do not take their voting freedoms lightly.

For many years, Northwest citizens had voted in a blanket Primary. In the blanket Primary, voters could skip across political party lines and select any candidate from any party for the upcoming November ballot. For example, a voter could choose a Republican candidate for Governor and a Democratic candidate for Attorney General on the same blanket Primary ballot. The lead candidates from each of the political parties would then appear on the ballot in the November General Election.

Adopted by initiative in 1935, the blanket Primary was extremely popular with voters at large, but strongly disliked by the state's major political parties. The parties championed a closed Primary that required voters to affiliate with a particular party, and only choose from that party's slate of candidates.

Washington's blanket Primary survived years of controversy and two State Supreme Court challenges before legal action elsewhere left it on slippery ground. Finally in February 2004, the U.S. Supreme Court let stand a lower court decision declaring California's blanket Primary unconstitutional. Because California's system was modeled after Washington's Primary, the court ruling triggered a lawsuit in the Northwest state. On September 15, 2003, the 9th Circuit Court of Appeals declared Washington's blanket Primary unconstitutional. For the first time in 70 years, the State of Washington had no legal Primary system in place.

"Political Parties: 1 - Washington Voters: 0" declared Kennewick's *Tri-City Herald.*[1]

"Blanket Primary Rejected as Unconstitutional" stated the *Seattle Times.*[2]

"Future Primaries in Doubt" reported the Tacoma *News Tribune.*[3]

The court ruling handed the State's legislature an awkward task that needed to be addressed quickly before the upcoming 2004 primary and general elections. They were charged with replacing a Primary system that was overwhelmingly popular with their own constituents. Citizens liked the ability to vote for candidates from either party in the traditional blanket Primary. To complicate matters further, the major political parties invested considerable resources to sway State decision makers toward a more restrictive Primary, requiring voters to affiliate with a particular party, and vote accordingly only in that party's slate of competing candidates.

Meanwhile, Secretary of State Sam Reed, who strongly opposed his own party on the issue, used the power of the bully pulpit, the news media, and legislative relations to defend a new system similar to the blanket Primary and one that the people of Washington would support.

"Primary Chaos in Washington" noted the national newspaper, *Roll Call,* on February 24, 2004.[4]

Tension began to build. Legislators, party activists, and key players at the Office of the Secretary of State worked on the Primary issue day and night. Reed recruited a sophisticated former Assistant Attorney General, Nick Handy, to educate the legislature.

Eventually, two kinds of primaries emerged for consideration. One style, the "top-two" Primary, would advance the top two vote getters, regardless of their political party affiliation, to the November election. (Potentially, though probably rather unlikely, this could result in two candidates from the same party appearing for a position on the November ballot, excluding candidates from the other party who lost in the Primary.) In the second, the "pick-a-party" Primary, voters were required to choose a political party slate and only vote for that party's candidates. This would ensure that one candidate from each major political party would appear on the November General Election ballot. Legislators were fairly evenly divided on the two proposals, such that neither side had support to pass a stand-alone bill.

The state's political party chairmen—the Democrat's Paul Berendt and the Republican's Chris Vance—strongly supported a "pick-a-party" Primary. Vance made it clear that the Republican Party would not endorse any Primary style that allowed a voter to choose candidates from either party. "That's the one thing that absolutely is not negotiable," Vance told the *Olympian*.[5]

The top-two Primary plan passed in the legislature, but with the pick-a-party Primary on its heels as a fallback. Thus, should a court of law toss out the top-two Primary, voters would cast their ballots in a pick-a-party Primary—no new legislation would be required.

Talk of a Governor's veto, however, spread throughout the capital. Reed, Lieutenant Governor Brad Owen, Commissioner of Public Lands Doug Sutherland, and key legislators wrote an open letter to Governor Gary Locke. "Your pending action on Washington's new Primary election system may be the most significant legacy of your governorship. The people of Washington and the 2004 Legislature have spoken on this issue."[6]

> *"Washington's new primary election system may be the most significant legacy of your governorship."*
> **—Statement sent to Gov. Locke**

On April Fools' Day, to the shock of the Office of the Secretary of State, Locke changed the course of the state's political history by vetoing the top-two Primary section of the bill and leaving the fallback, pick-a-party Primary firmly in place. The veto stunned many who felt it an affront to voters and legislators, who mainly supported a more open Primary.

But Locke stood firm—maintaining his veto was the only way to guarantee that voters would have a choice between a Democratic and Republican candidate for all the contests in the November general elections.

"Locke Rewrites Primary Election Law with Veto Pen" noted Spokane's *Spokesman-Review*.[7]

"This veto hurts the voters of this state," said Secretary Reed. "Killing the top-two primary takes away the public's right to vote for the person, not the party and threatens our proud history of independence."[8]

Litigation immediately ensued questioning the legality of Locke's veto. In June 2004, the court upheld the veto, and as a result, also Washington's new pick-a-party Primary.

Preparations for the Pick-a-Party Primary

The late decision sent the elections community and the Secretary of State's Office scrambling to prepare for an unpopular Primary. In a matter of only weeks, elections workers raced to train poll site staff, reprogram ballot-tabulation devices, prepare for a complex, multiple-ballot format, and meet other technical challenges.

> *"During the Florida debacle in 2000, the entire nation learned the importance of voter education."*
>
> **—Sam Reed, press release, August 12, 2004.**

Public education quickly became a top priority. Since the Secretary of State oversees elections in Washington, the voter education effort ironically fell to Reed, who had advocated against the pick-a-party Primary plan.

"During the Florida debacle in 2000, the entire nation learned the importance of voter education," said Reed. "Two years later Congress passed legislation, the *Help America Vote Act*, paying for and mandating extensive voter education in every state. Washington has a brand new primary in 2004. And we're doing everything we can to inform voters and protect their right to vote."[9]

The Office of the Secretary of State assembled a team to lead a wide-ranging, aggressive media campaign in what was largely a public political minefield. Team members included Assistant Secretary of State Steve Excell, Assistant Director of Elections Erika Aust, Communications Director Trova Heffernan, Communications Manager Bobbie Egan, Elections Policy Analyst Shawn Merchant, and Coordinator Justin Anderson.

Jones Advertising, based in Seattle, came up with a clever approach to diffuse the political pressure cooker, winning the contract for the statewide ad campaign. The visual media spots featured each major political party's symbol—a donkey, an elephant, and "Lady Liberty," representing the Democratic, Republican, and Libertarian parties respectively.

"The message is clear, and we believe it will resonate well with voters," Reed announced the week before the ads were released. Reed humorously added: "The woman who plays Lady Liberty, the elephant, and the donkey all met our expectations. We're especially amazed at the animals' talent and their ability to walk into a voting

Office of the Secretary of State

booth on command and even pick up a pencil."[10]

The ads starred a donkey, Lady Liberty played by an actor, and a six-ton elephant named Nellie, skilled enough to pick up a pencil with her trunk. The message was simple: choose Republican, choose Democratic, or choose Libertarian, but only pick candidates from one political party. At the same time, the Secretary of State's Office mailed a pamphlet to each voter, announcing the Primary changes and explaining the new system as simply and clearly as possible.

After the $1.7 million campaign was launched, the team quickly realized one element had been underestimated—voters were angry about the new Primary, and widespread discontent boiled over. The good news was that the campaign was effective and voters now understood the new Primary system. But the bad news was exactly the same: Voters now understood the nature of the new Primary.

"What idiot came up with the new rule that we vote for one party?" wrote Mike Williams in a fiery email to Reed.[11]

Phone calls and email flooded election offices across the state. The fact that a U.S. Supreme Court decision, State legislative action, and a surprising Governor's veto had changed Washington's Primary system was lost on most voters. Irate constituents simply wanted no part of the new pick-a-party Primary and personally held Reed and county auditors responsible.

Reed became worried that people would protest the new Primary by refusing to vote.

"SHAME on you for allowing the political parties to take you to this point. On this issue your office does a DISSERVICE to the voting public! It seems to boil down to the almighty dollar and who has the most influence!" remarked Marian Ely.[12]

"I would like to know who the hell you think you are? You are taking my rights," wrote Lori Young of Moxee City.[13]

"I just wanted to state on behalf of my husband and I, that we are first time voters this year and it will probably be the last time if the new law stays in effect," said Victoria and Don Riche.[14]

Reed called a press conference urging people to put their reactions aside and vote in September. "People are angry and they want to know how this happened," said Reed. "As the chief elections officer, I have a responsibility to tell them and to urge every registered voter in this state to take part in the September 14 primaries and put their emotions aside for the day."[15]

At the height of the protest, the office received an email from an angry voter every 30 seconds and 2,000 phone calls in a 24-hour time period. Temporary workers were hired to help manage this unprecedented onslaught.

Despite the controversy, the intense public education effort paid off. The public did turn out to vote, and the new pick-a-party Primary brought few surprises on election day. According to a survey of voters conducted by the Office of the Secretary of State on the day of the Primary—

- 98 percent were aware of the new system before arriving to vote.
- 75 percent found casting their ballot somewhat easy or very easy; 24 percent found it somewhat or very confusing.
- 94 percent recognized the non-partisan races.
- 38 percent said it took longer than usual to vote; 57 percent said it took about the same amount of time.
- 58 percent had a negative or very negative reaction to the single party ballot; 21 percent had a positive or very positive reaction to the single party ballot.
- 70 percent were confident or very confident that no record was kept of their confidential ballot (party) selection.
- 84 percent were confident or very confident that their vote was accurately recorded and counted.
- 53 percent would have voted for a candidate but could not because he or she was on a different ballot than the one they chose.
- 59 percent opposed the new Primary system.

Positive editorials followed.

> **"Less Confusion than First Thought in Thurston County Election"** noted the *News Tribune.*[16]
>
> **"Larger Turnout, Less Confusion Reported in New-Ballot Primary"** said Seattle's *Post-Intelligencer.*[17]

The entire elections community let out a collective sigh of relief. It appeared the most difficult challenges had been met. The political season carried on toward November—business as usual. Campaign signs began littering roadway intersections, and political ads filled the air waves. And at water

Impact of America's Most Disputed U.S. Presidential Election

Bold Election Reform Sweeps the Nation

In addition to the controversial new pick-a-party Primary, State election administers began preparing for a dramatic package of election reforms resulting from one of the most contentious Presidential races in history.

The U.S. Congress passed the *Help America Vote Act* (HAVA) in response to the disputed 2000 U.S. Presidential election in Florida. The act assigned election administrators with difficult and complex responsibilities. While many requirements would not become effective until 2005 or 2006, the new obligations required substantial preparation.

Among the changes, the *Help America Vote Act* provided sight impaired voters a truly secret ballot for the first time. Under HAVA, Washington's counties were required to provide disability access devices by 2006. Using these special machines, sight-impaired voters could wear headphones and listen as a recorded voice guided them through the ballot. In addition, HAVA mandated that counties replace punch card voting machines, and that the State merge 39 county voter registration lists into a single, statewide database.

Another important HAVA provision effective in 2004 required states to establish a "fail-safe," or provisional, ballot. Provisional ballots were important because they ensured that no voter was denied the right to vote. The State of Washington had provided these special ballots for years. As a result, no Washington citizen has been turned away from any poll site because his or her name "did not appear" on a precinct list of registered voters. Because of Washington's prior experience with these ballots, and because almost no difficulties had occurred with provisional ballots in the past, election officials were not expecting major issues with this new HAVA requirement in either the primary or general elections of 2004.

Unforeseen was the degree to which the provisional ballot would be used in 2004, especially during the General Election because political parties actively promoted them. Due to the vague nature of the new federal requirements on provisional voting, states interpreted the language differently. In some states, a voter actually had to live within the precinct at which he or she attempted to vote to receive a provisional ballot. Other states interpreted these requirements differently. In Washington, a voter registered in one county could be issued a provisional ballot at another county's polling place. The ballot would be subsequently forwarded to the appropriate county and votes would only be counted for those issues and candidates for which the person was entitled to vote.

coolers everywhere, voters grumbled over traditional politics.

Little did anyone realize, the stage was set for the closest governor's race in American history.

Endnotes

1. *Tri-City Herald,* September 16, 2003.
2. Susan Gilmore, *Seattle Times,* September 16, 2003.
3. Joe Turner, *News Tribune,* September 16, 2003.
4. Nicole Duran, *Roll Call,* February 24, 2004.
5. Brad Shannon, "Legislators Narrow Primary Gap," *Olympian,* February 27, 2004.
6. Reed et al. to Governor Gary Locke, March 16, 2004.
7. Richard Roesler, *Spokesman-Review,* April 2, 2004.
8. Office of the Secretary of State, "Reed Responds to Governor's Veto of the Primary Bill," media statement, April 1, 2004.
9. Office of the Secretary of State, "Reed Announces a New Primary Education Campaign," press release, August 12, 2004.
10. Ibid.
11. Mike Williams, email, August 22, 2004.
12. Marian Ely, email, August 23, 2004.
13. Lori Young, email, August 23, 2004.
14. Victoria and Don Riche, email, August 24, 2004.
15. Office of the Secretary of State, "Reed Addresses Public Anger over New Primary, Encourages Citizens to Vote September 14," press release, August 24, 2004.
16. Associated Press, *News Tribune,* September 15, 2004.
17. Neil Modie and Lewis Dam, *Post-Intelligencer,* September 15, 2004.

Political analysts noted the electorate slowly dividing between the two main candidates.

Chapter Two

Dreams of a Governorship

In 2004, the parade of contenders hoping to win the hearts of voters and gain the Governor's office included six Democrats, three Republicans, and two Libertarians. Only three made the quantum leap onto the public's radar—a Republican rising star, a nationally recognized State Attorney General, and an affable King County Chief Executive.

Ron Sims

Office of Secretary of State

Ron Sims was one of two viable Democratic candidates. Famous for his gregarious manner and charming, dynamic oratory, Sims held the top spot in King County government as its chief executive. In his own words, Sims built his political career on "the progressive principles of social justice, good government, and environmental stewardship."[1]

The well-known Democrat, originally from Spokane, promised leadership and solutions for Washington. For too long, Sims claimed, the citizens of eastern Washington "have been relegated to the kids' table in Olympia."[2] As Governor, Sims vowed to revitalize the economy. He stumped for a state income tax and gay marriage.

Christine Gregoire

Office of Secretary of State

In the Primary, Sims faced the candidate many considered most viable of all—Democrat and three-term Attorney General Christine Gregoire. She was raised in the small town of Auburn, tucked in the Green River Valley. Washington voters knew Gregoire well. She had been the first woman elected as State Attorney General. Of all the state attorneys general taking on the tobacco companies in 1998, it was Gregoire, a lead negotiator in the national discussion, who was most credited with inking the multi-billion-dollar deal. Gregoire was articulate, bright, and of the gender with a political advantage in Washington State—a female.

Even before filing for office, Gregoire was at the top of her political game and appeared to be a shoe-in for the Democratic nomination. Early polling gave her a sizable lead over Sims. In a mid-July telephone poll of

600 "likely" voters, she was up by 31 points (52 to 21 percent).[3]

Her political life and personal life collided, however, when days after announcing her candidacy for Governor, she was diagnosed with breast cancer. Determined to run, the mother of two stayed in the race and promised, among other things, healthcare insurance for low-income children.

Dino Rossi

Office of Secretary of State

In the minds of many voters, Dino Rossi had a reputation as a fiscal conservative with a social conscience, whose politics fell generally near the center of the political spectrum. The Republican candidate pledged to return accountability to the Governor's Office, revitalize the economy, and create jobs.

A rising star in state politics, Rossi carried the hope of his party in the palm of his hand. For the first time in years, Republican Party insiders could almost taste victory. With this charming and successful standard-bearer, Washington's top seat seemed well within reach.

In many ways, Dino Rossi lived the American dream. A married father of four, he was a self-made real estate entrepreneur. In State politics, Rossi chaired the State Senate Ways and Means Committee. His greatest feat was balancing Washington's 2003 budget.

On the campaign trail, the Sammamish area resident focused on his humble upbringing and the conversation with his wife that convinced him to subject his family to the demands and scrutiny of a statewide gubernatorial campaign. Nevertheless, next to Gregoire, most political analysts would have considered Rossi the undisputed underdog, but undeniably, his message was penetrating and his popularity began to rise.

The Primary Campaign

Typically during a Presidential election year, Washington voters are especially inundated by the competing campaigns' claims of political scandal, mudslinging, and implications of character assassination. The 2004 Primary was no exception. Of the three viable candidates, however, Rossi escaped strong opposition in the Primary. As a result, it was much easier for the Republican favorite to hang onto his war chest and maintain his image.

Christine Gregoire and Ron Sims were not so lucky.

The $18 Million Mistake

On April 18, 2004, readers of the *Seattle Times* woke up to a potentially damning story regarding Christine Gregoire. Four years before, a jury ordered the state to pay almost $18 million in a civil case involving a State-licensed facility and three disabled men. An attorney from Gregoire's Attorney General's Office missed the deadline to appeal. The mistake left taxpayers with a record bill. Gregoire paid for an independent review to assess the botched case, but media reports in April suggested the reviewers had been improperly influenced.

The *Seattle Times* claimed: "Gregoire's staff shaped 'independent' investigation."[4]

According to a *Times* reporter, the Sims' campaign provided information for the story. The *Times* article justified the source and its publishing of these findings. "Most sources don't call to dish the dirt on their friends. It comes from opponents and enemies. Reporters have to factor in motive and spin, but believe me, if we dismissed everything because it came from an opponent, there'd be lots of white space in the paper. There's not a candidate who doesn't play that game."[5]

Claims of Discrimination

Gregoire's troubles did not end there. On August 23, less than a month before the Primary, a story broke linking the gubernatorial contender to racism decades earlier.

In 1966 when she was 19 years old, college-bound Christine Gregoire pledged with the Kappa Delta sorority at the University of Washington. During those times, some Seattle organizations still practiced racial exclusion, including the Kappa Delta sorority, which followed a whites-only policy.

Gregoire claimed she initially was unaware of the policy banning people of color and had considered leaving. But she remained, and became the sorority's president. After graduating, Gregoire said she tried to persuade the sorority's national conference to drop the exclusion. The rule ultimately was eliminated, but some time after Gregoire's efforts.

Sims, an African-American, did not comment directly on this issue, but many in the African-American community did. Carl Mack, president of the Seattle chapter of the National Association for the Advancement of Colored People, was outspoken and blunt in his criticism of Gregoire. "You sit silently in a sorority and now, today, you come out and say you were a champion for civil rights; that's hard to swallow."[6]

Despite the intense criticism, Gregoire's campaign prevailed over both the bungled legal case and the accusations of racism.

The Primary Vote

Washington voters turned out in high numbers on September 14, 2004, for the new pick-a-party Primary and selected their choices for Governor. When the Secretary of State certified the results, Rossi had won the Republican Primary handily—with 444,337 votes, or 85 percent of all Republican votes cast. Gregoire won the Democratic Primary with 504,018 votes, or 65.6 percent, whereas Ron Sims took nearly 30 percent.

The Libertarian Lawsuit

On September 28, Libertarians filed a lawsuit hoping to add gubernatorial candidate Ruth Bennett and U.S. Senate candidate J. Mills to the November ballot. Under State law, a candidate must receive at least 1 percent of the total votes cast in the State Primary to qualify for the November election. While J. Mills just missed clearing the 1 percent vote threshold, Bennett missed the mark by a wider margin.

In their lawsuit, the Libertarians' argued that the 1 percent requirement was unconstitutional because it violated the equal protection rights of minor parties. They claimed both candidates should appear on the November ballot. The State called for a dismissal, arguing the case had no basis and that the General Election was quickly approaching.

A Three-Way Affair

On September 29, Thurston County Superior Court Judge Richard Strophy advanced Mills and Bennett to the General Election ballot. Strophy ruled that the new "pick-a-party" primary rendered the 1 percent requirement unconstitutional. He applied his ruling to Mills and Bennett only, and to no other Libertarian candidates.

The Spokane Case

In the week following the Ruth Bennett decision, other Libertarian candidates in Spokane County filed suit against the Spokane County Auditor, also seeking access to the General Election ballot. These candidates made the same arguments. However, in this case, the 1 percent requirement was held constitutional and ballot access was denied.

With no time for the State to appeal, the Governor's race became a three-way affair overnight.

The General Election Campaign

As the General Election neared, the gubernatorial candidates prepared for the fight of their political lives. Campaign signs appeared across the state, posted on fence posts in small towns and roadway intersections in urban areas.

A mid-September poll conducted by Stuart Elway showed that Gregoire held an 11 point lead (49 to 38 percent) and dominated much of the state except the Republican stronghold of eastern Washington. There, Rossi was up 56 to 41 percent. The poll also revealed that Independents favored Gregoire over Rossi by a margin of 49 to 26 percent.[7]

But as the intensity of the race began to build, political analysts noted the electorate slowly dividing closer between the two main candidates.

Rossi Campaign

Meanwhile on the campaign trail, Rossi focused on the record of 20 years of Democratic governing, which he claimed drove the state into deep economic troubles. The missed filing deadline for the $18 million judgment surfaced again in broadcast and print ads, along with allegations of other mismanagement during Gregoire's tenure as Attorney General.

The Rossi campaign called her an Olympia insider, and more likely to exacerbate than solve Washington's financial problems. At the same time, broadcast ads depicted Rossi as a successful businessman, a devoted family man, and a moderate.

Gregoire Campaign

Democrats portrayed Gregoire as a centrist and emphasized her $4.5 billion win for Washington against "Big Tobacco." The Gregoire camp criticized Rossi for a conservative voting record, claiming it was far different from his "centrist" gubernatorial campaign message. They also claimed he worked against *Roe v. Wade*. Rossi's professional association with a real estate broker convicted of fraud surfaced, along with allegations of embellishments in Rossi's resume.

Justice Department Warnings

On September 29, Secretary of State Sam Reed received a stern warning from the U.S. Department of Justice—if Washington failed to mail out General Election ballots to military personnel on time, the State could be sued. "We will not hesitate to take legal action if necessary to make sure that overseas voters are not disenfranchised," warned the Justice Department.[1]

Federal law required service ballots to be mailed 30 days before November's General Election, but Washington's late Primary held in mid-September made it difficult to meet the deadline. However, because State law required absentee ballots to be mailed 18 days before the General Election, and because returned service ballots could be received 15 days after the General Election, the State considered the 30-day ballot transit requirement satisfied. The Department of Justice disagreed.

Eventually, a settlement was reached to mail the service ballots out by Friday, October 8. This was 23 days before the General Election and one week before all absentee ballots would be mailed. The State met the deadline and no litigation followed. In fact, in 2004 more than 37,000 General Election mail ballots were sent to military and overseas citizens—81 percent were returned.

1. R. Alexander Acosta, Assistant Attorney General, U.S. Department of Justice, to Secretary of State Sam Reed, September 29, 2004.

Home Stretch

Less than two weeks before the General Election, Gregoire's lead slipped. According to an October report in the *Seattle Weekly*, only 6 points now separated Gregoire from Rossi (48 to 42 percent; *Strategic Vision*).

An analysis published in *The Elway Report* concluded that "attack ads" against Gregoire were resonating with voters. Though many voters had yet to commit to Rossi, they were no longer supporting his Democratic opponent. The shift was undeniable.

A *Seattle Weekly* article entitled "Armageddon for the GOP" reported that Jennifer Duffy of *The Cook Report* changed her analysis of the Governor's race based on national trends from "leaning Democratic" to "tossup."

The Final Days

Just before the November 2 election, supporters in both camps clung to optimism.

Turnout predictions ran as high as 84 percent due in part to a get-out-the-vote campaign sweeping the country. Many analysts believed a high turnout would work in Gregoire's favor. "When you get above 80 percent, that's dangerous for any Republican," said a Republican strategist.[8]

Meanwhile, Rossi supporters held high hopes when hearing encouraging rumors that internal tracking polls put the two contenders in a dead heat. Newspaper editorial sections were divided in their advocacy of the main candidates. Five daily newspapers, including the *Seattle Times*, supported Rossi, while six newspapers, including Seattle*'s Post-Intelligencer*, favored Gregoire.

The timing of election day itself may have had something to do with the incredible dead-even split that resulted. Some speculate that November 2 was the precise moment when the public was perfectly divided between the two candidates.

Under this assumption, had the election been held one day earlier, on November 1, Gregoire would have won without recounts and subsequent court hearings. Had the election been held a day later, on November 3, Rossi would have won without recounts and court involvement.

Endnotes

1. Ron Sims, Your.KingCounty.gov/exec/about.aspx.
2. Richard Roesler, "Spokane Native Sims Joins Race," *Spokesman-Review,* July 30, 2003.
3. Mellman Group Poll of Likely Voters, July 14–17, 2004.
4. Ralph Thomas and Janet I. Tu, "African-American Leaders Aim Criticism at Gregoire," *Seattle Times,* August 25, 2004.
5. Ibid.
6. Ibid.
7. David Postman, "Digging Up Dirt, Tossing It Around," *Seattle Times,* September 29, 2004.
8. George Howland Jr., "Armageddon for the GOP," *Seattle Weekly,* October 27, 2004.

I've never seen such partisan polarization—and mobilization.

Chapter Three

The Horse Race Makes History

The unprecedented "get-out-the-vote" effort that swept across the nation on November 2, 2004, lost no momentum in Washington State. The political parties organized thousands of volunteers, who in turn contacted many thousands of other voters. Dedicated campaigners lined the state's busiest intersections, stumping for candidates one last time.

"I've never seen such partisan polarization—and mobilization," declared political scientist Todd Donovan of Western Washington University in Bellingham.[1]

Secretary of State Sam Reed was up early reviewing his prediction that Washington would make history on this day—if 84 out of every 100 registered voters cast ballots. Reed's calculation would mark the highest percentage turnout since World War II.

"The political pot has been stirred and voters are motivated," Reed had been telling reporters for weeks. "This state is a battleground for the Presidency; the Democratic and Republican candidates for Governor are polling in a statistical dead heat."[2]

The large turnout resulted from the notable get-out-the-vote drives and considerable campaign donations. Rossi and Gregoire's gubernatorial campaigns raised a combined total of $12.6 million.

The parties were motivated. The Democrats were determined to keep claim to the Governor's Mansion, which had been Democratic turf since Republican John Spellman was ousted in 1984. But the Republicans were equally motivated, thanks to their star candidate who shook up a race previously considered an easy win for Gregoire. Rossi seemed the perfect fit to finally break the Democrats' hold on the Governor's Office.

This was just one race on the ballot, of course. In addition to a new Governor, Washington voters would vote for a President (Kerry vs. Bush), a U.S. Senator, and nine members of Congress. Without question, the 2004 election was packed with big decisions.

It also brought with it baggage from the contested Gore-Bush Presidential race of 2000. Still reeling from the Florida debacle four years before, Washington's political parties were highly suspicious of the entire voting process. They stationed some 600 lawyers across the state on the hunt for any anomalies.[3]

"I hope there won't be any problems. There never have been in Washington State," Republican Party Chairman Chris Vance told the *Post-*

Many Washington voters supported three Democratic women for the State's most prominent offices. As this picture was taken, Maria Cantwell (left) and Patty Murray (right) securely held their U.S. Senate positions. Only the fate of Christine Gregoire as Governor remained in question. Gregoire was preparing for the political fight of her life.
Alan Berner/The Seattle Times

Intelligencer on October 30. "But this is what Florida has done to all of us… It makes us paranoid. It makes us armed to the teeth and prepared for the worst."[4]

Behind the scenes, election offices across the state began the enormous undertaking of tabulating ballots. Although no results would be reported until after the polls closed at 8 p.m., the validation of signatures, the crediting of voters, and the sorting of ballots by type had started—activities that would take election workers more than two weeks to complete.

When the polls closed, restless voters waited for results. Meanwhile, the two popular candidates for the State's top post kept their supporters enthused, while holding any nagging doubts private.

At the Democrats' gathering at Seattle's Westin Hotel that evening, a memorable photograph was taken of gubernatorial candidate Christine Gregoire and U.S. senators Maria Cantwell and Patty Murray. Cantwell still had two years to go before she would run for office again and Murray had just eased toward a decisive win, but Christine Gregoire's greatest challenge was still to come. "I'm coming back down here as the next governor of the great state of Washington," a poised and determined Gregoire announced to a room full of cheering supporters.[5]

Less than a half-hour's drive away at the Meydenbauer Center in Bellevue, Gregoire's opponent energized a full house with just as much confidence. "We are trending in the right direction," announced an inspired Dino Rossi, holding his daughter in front of a Republican crowd.[6]

"We feel very, very good," said Republican Party Chairman Chris Vance. "It's not a done deal but…you can tell that this crowd is about to go nuts."[7]

After the crowds thinned out and election-night counts were wrapping up, Gregoire and Rossi were locked in a drum-tight race.

With more than 90 percent of the precincts reporting statewide, Gregoire led Rossi by roughly 4,000 votes out of some 1.8 million counted so far.

Predictably, Gregoire held strong in Seattle and King County, capturing about 58 percent of the vote to Rossi's 40 percent. Also as expected, she won four other counties in the Puget Sound region. Just as predictably, Rossi prevailed elsewhere, and by sizable margins in a number of eastern Washington counties.

As ballots were counted that night, Rossi had 916,395 votes, Gregoire 915,714, and Ruth Bennett 39,065. Rossi, once declared the undisputed underdog, had now taken the lead by a remarkably close 681 votes. There was no question—the GOP had a fighting chance for the Governor's Mansion for the first time in years.

But there still were many votes to count. An estimated 848,019 ballots still needed to be counted and 357,000 of them were cast in King County. This was not unusual. Typically, as many as 70 percent of voters statewide cast mail ballots, and many voters wait until the last minute to send them. Washington is a "postmark" state, meaning the ballots can be postmarked and sent up to the day of the election.

As a result, ballots would stream into elections offices for two more weeks, particularly from overseas. Meanwhile, the candidates, political parties, and voters would sit on pins and needles waiting for the final tabulation.

Furthermore, each of the ballots in the "provisional" category needed to be individually researched, and when found valid, duplicated to a proper ballot in only the races that a person was entitled to vote. (The provisional ballot process is time consuming, and typically finalized at the end of the tallying process.)

In other words, the deciding votes in the 2004 gubernatorial race were still making their way through the mail. The next morning, uncertainty clouded the race. The Rossi-Gregoire contest had ended in a dead heat. As the *Seattle Weekly* pointed out, the equally split electorate had done it again. "When you blend Democratic blue and Republican red, you get purple, and Washington voters turned out in record numbers

Changing Ballot Estimates Create Suspicion

While the public anxiously followed every development in the tight race, changing announced estimates in the number of ballots left to be counted caused suspicion among many. Ballot estimates were only partly based on the number of ballots on hand. It also was based on the number of outstanding ballots that might be returned, an estimated number of provisional ballots (given to voters who do not appear on the poll books, often due to moving their residence to another county), and an estimate of the number of ballots that needed some sort of resolution before tabulation.

The shifting number of ballots fueled controversy. Some alleged ballots were mysteriously being added to the "ballots to be counted," changing the outcome of the race. With King County voting 60 percent for Gregoire, 10,000 more ballots to count would be extrapolated as plus 2,000 votes for Gregoire over Rossi.

Tuesday, November 2, to affirm their constitutional right to mix colors."[8]

"Except for the counting—and, perhaps, the lawsuits—it's finally over. Our roadways (soon, we hope) will be free of political signs, our airwaves liberated from the now-grating phrase 'and I approve this message,'" noted the *Everett Herald*.[9]

By 8:30 a.m., November 3, the Secretary of State's Office began preparations for a possible recount. The Communications Office briefed the news media on the State's recount laws, history, and trends. An hour later, Secretary Reed began the first of a dozen interviews to keep reporters apprised of the possibilities.

In an email to the Communications Office, Elections Director Nick Handy explained that as many as 90,000 provisional ballots may have been issued.

"Assuming we still have about 800,000 to 900,000 ballots to count, that means provisional ballots could be in the ten percent range of outstanding ballots. Provisional ballots are of interest for several reasons that cut both ways in the Governor's race.

"(1) They will get counted last (no particular benefit to either candidate);

"(2) They may tend to include more college students and thus a more liberal vote (perhaps favoring Gregoire); and

"(3) As an election day ballot, provisional ballots are also a 'later' ballot more subject to trending activity (in this case, later ballots are perceived as trending toward Rossi as he was narrowing the gap in the opinion polls)."[10]

This internal communication between Handy, the executive staff, and Reed intensified as another dozen counties were scheduled to count ballots throughout the day.

November 3—Gregoire by 14,333

By the close of the day on November 3, Gregoire claimed her first substantial lead—14,323 votes. Collectively, Washington's 39 counties reported the following:

Gregoire	980,190 votes
Rossi	965,867 votes
Bennett	41,434 votes

In the counties, an estimated 795,595 ballots were left to be counted. The lead accumulated by Gregoire, however, could be directly traced to 96,000 absentee ballots in populous King County, a Gregoire stronghold. Outside of King County, Gregoire led in Whatcom, San Juan, Jefferson, Thurston, Grays Harbor, Pacific, and Cowlitz counties. Rossi dominated the 31 other, mostly rural, counties. Washington's urban-rural divide was as evident as ever.

Despite lagging in the count, the Republicans were optimistic. "It's looking good," said Mary Lane, a spokeswoman for Rossi. "There are about 100,000 more outstanding [absentee] ballots in pro-Rossi counties than in pro-Gregoire counties."[11]

Both campaigns settled in for the long, tense days lying ahead. "All you can do is watch at this point," said the Republicans' Chris Vance. "You can't influence it anymore."[12] Both parties trained volunteers to monitor the absentee counts in each county.

Voters Bid Farewell to Washington's Pick-a-Party Primary

Voters in 2004 may have been divided over Washington's next Governor, but they decisively tossed out the pick-a-party Primary when approving Initiative 872. Sponsored by the Washington State Grange, the initiative passed 59.8 to 40.1 percent.

Initiative 872 replaced the pick-a-party Primary with a new system whereby the top two vote getters advanced to the November election, regardless of their political party affiliation. Voters could choose any candidate on the Primary ballot.

"It's a lot of standing around drinking coffee, watching people count ballots," Christian Sinderman, a Gregoire adviser, said. "It's not just a frustrating process. It's a boring process."[13]

All realized Washington's next Governor would claim office by the thinnest of margins. Keeping plenty of eyes on the voting process was common logic.

November 5—Gregoire by 4,001

The margin narrowed on November 4 and 5, when new vote totals dropped Gregoire's lead to 4,001 votes:

Gregoire	1,192,259
Rossi	1,188,258
Bennett	52,318

County auditors now reported 362,246 ballots yet to be counted, with

Special Ballots and Voter Privacy

Across the country, the question arose among state election directors as to whether or not names and addresses of voters casting provisional ballots could be made publicly available under the provisions of the *Help America Vote Act,* Section 302(a). At least one state—Maryland—took the position that these voters were protected from public disclosure under language in HAVA.

According to Reed's attorneys, HAVA did not clearly address the issue. Any county asked to release this information, they advised, should consult its prosecuting attorney. The discussion continued within the elections community, with no consensus reached.

an estimated 119,000 in King County. Among the total number of outstanding ballots, an estimated 88,000 were provisional, issued to voters on election day.[14]

The close race for Governor increasingly stirred interest. Political junkies punched calculators at a feverish pitch, exploiting every imaginable scenario based on how the outstanding ballots, by their geographic distribution, would impact the final vote. Their attention was given to the prior voting patterns of various localities. Prognostications also were made about how provisional votes might trend.

Historically, Washington's absentee voters were older people who tended to favor Republicans. But this pattern now was diluted by a growing, broader range of people voting by mail. The old stereotype was changing. Nevertheless, because Rossi had gained increasing support toward the end of the campaign, many assumed that ballots sent on election day were more likely to benefit him.

November 8—Gregoire by 8,736

Meanwhile, counties continued to report results. After the next significant counting of ballots on Monday, November 8, Gregoire increased her lead to 8,736 votes.

Gregoire	1,262,590
Rossi	1,253,854
Bennett	55,683

Counties now estimated there were 213,110 ballots left to count. Both campaigns found reason for optimism. Gregoire held her lead, as she had since November 3, but more ballots remained to be counted in pro-Rossi than in pro-Gregoire counties.

November 9—Rossi by 2,000

Twenty-four hours later the tables turned on Gregoire. She lost her slim lead when 56,000 ballots from pro-Rossi counties were added to the mix. The switch put Dino Rossi in a 2,000 vote lead. "We're very happy with these numbers, but, with that in

Secretary Reed takes reporters' questions as news of the race changes by the hour.
Office of the Secretary of State

mind, we still have to wait until all the votes are counted," said Lane, Rossi's spokeswoman.[15]

"We expected to end the day down between 6,000 and 8,000" votes, said Morton Brilliant, Gregoire's spokesman. "We view [the actual margin] as good news. We look forward to King [County] and the rest of the state tomorrow."[16]

November 10—Rossi by 3,500

However, Gregoire did not come out on top during the next count. After adding 82,000 ballots on November 10—including 21,000 in King County—Rossi actually widened his lead to 3,500 votes.

In addition, among the 85,000 remaining ballots to count, the *Post-Intelligencer* noted that "only 31,000 are in the seven counties where Gregoire leads."[17] The news brought public criticism of the Gregoire campaign. "Whether she wins or loses, Democrats have to be disappointed by the performance of their candidate," wrote reporter George Howland for the *Seattle Weekly.* "What happened? The conventional wisdom is that Rossi successfully repeated his simple message of 'change' with positive advertising, while the GOP relentlessly pounded Gregoire on the failure, under her watch, of the attorney general's office to appeal a $17.8 million verdict against the state.

"Gregoire, in turn, did not make an impression on the electorate. By the end of the campaign, nobody knew what she stood for or what she was going to do."[18]

In fact, the *Seattle Times* reported that Dino Rossi already was choosing his transition staff.

"While the race remained much too close to call, Rossi yesterday announced his transition team. He said the public needs to know that the eventual winner of the governor's race is prepared to take over.

"'We don't know if we've won. We don't know if we've lost. We've got to be prepared,' Rossi said.

"State Democratic Party Chairman Paul Berendt called Rossi's announcement 'presumptuous.'

"But Gregoire is also making transition plans. She said in a written statement that she would not discuss them publicly until the race is decided 'because I don't want to overshadow the ongoing vote count.'"[19]

November 12—Rossi by 1,920; King County Court Rules for Democrats

On Friday, November 12, the King County returns were headed to court. The Democratic Party had sought names and addresses of voters whose provisional ballots were ruled invalid, but King County refused to turn them over.

The ballots had been deemed invalid because the voters casting them were not registered, or their signatures did not match those on file at the county elections department. King County, acting on the advice of its prosecuting attorney, took the position that federal law—specifically the *Help America Vote Act* (2002)—prohibited the release of such information.

The Democratic Party, of course, was vitally interested in increasing the number of ballots counted in King County. Assuming a continued 60 to 40 percent margin there for Gregoire, increasing the county ballot count by 100 voters could mean plus 20 votes for Gregoire. Increasing the vote count by 1,000 voters could mean plus 200 for Gregoire. In addition, the Democratic Party projected that voters who cast provisional ballots were more likely to have voted for Gregoire. In this effort, Democrats wanted to contact those voters who had their provisional ballots rejected and see about having them validated.

In court, they maintained that other counties were releasing this information, allowing voters to appeal the rejection of their ballots. Paul Berendt, the Democratic Party chair, claimed that of the 20 counties that did this, 19 favored Rossi.[20]

Specifically, the Democrats alleged that by refusing to turn over the information, King County was violating constitutional equal-protection and public disclosure rules. Attorney William Rava, arguing on their behalf, stated that the county was following a wrong interpretation of federal law.[21] The Democrats argued that counties regularly contacted "absentee" voters whose signatures were missing and that the same rules should apply for "provisional" ballots.

King County countered that the two types of ballots, absentee and provisional, were different. In the case of an absentee ballot, the voter was registered or the voter would not have received an absentee ballot at all. The same could not be said for a provisional ballot voter. (People receive provisional ballots because their status as registered voters is in question.)

Predictably, the Republican Party took a different view, charging that their political rivals were drumming up controversy. "I'm now becoming very worried that the Democrats are going to try and turn this into Florida," said

Chris Vance. "They're losing and now they're grasping at straws."[22]

Late on Friday afternoon, November 12, the King County Election Department lost in court and faced a 5 p.m. deadline to turn over 929 names of voters with disqualified ballots. According to Berendt, the Democrats would work through the weekend to notify those voters and see if their signature problems could be rectified and their votes counted.[23]

According to the *Post-Intelligencer,* the Democrats did, in fact, turn in affidavits and registration forms for 400 King County voters with problems in their provisional ballots, and planned to submit an additional 200.

The whole notion that a political party could inform voters about their rejected ballots and urge them to appeal was controversial. But King County now decided, on advice of counsel, that no prohibition existed in law regarding the involvement of third parties in this process. King County would accept such signatures.

Several news accounts indicated, however, that Democratic Party workers inquired how a person voted in the Governor's race. Allegedly, voters who supported Gregoire were offered assistance while Rossi voters were not. Some allegations went so far as to claim that documents collected from Rossi voters were tossed out by the Democratic workers. These sensational accusations only intensified an already emotionally charged political environment.

The Secretary of State opposed the practice of political parties going door-to-door in attempting to correct bad signatures on ballots. Reed was most concerned about the potential for abuse, and the unreliable information that inevitably would circulate if third parties were involved. (The Secretary proposed legislation the next year, clarifying that county auditors alone handle communication with voters if there were problems with verifying their signatures.)

By the end of the day when the lawsuit was filed and decided (November 12), new numbers indicated Gregoire was closing in on Rossi, whose lead was reduced to 1,920 votes.

Rossi	1,347,865
Gregoire	1,345,945
Bennett	61,349

Counties estimated 41,623 ballots were left to count; 11,000 of these in King County.

November 15—Gregoire by 158

By Monday, November 15, the counties had 48 hours left before certifying their final results (to occur on November 17).

With the Governor's contest being so close, the Office of the Secretary of State began discussions to obtain outside counsel regarding possible future litigation by the parties. Since Attorney General Gregoire was a candidate in the Governor's race and her staff also served as the attorneys for the

Secretary of State, all agreed representation from State lawyers was out of the question.

Preliminary discussions centered on the same firm, Davis Wright Tremaine, that represented Secretary Reed during litigation over Governor Locke's veto of the top-two primary. Davis Wright Tremaine already had agreed to represent the Republican Party in future litigation.

Meanwhile, the Secretary of State's Office issued a memorandum to county auditors on November 15, detailing procedures to be followed in the event of a call for a recount in the Governor's race. Included in the memorandum were sections covering county certification of the election results (to occur November 17), and the timing of a recount order if it came and a summary of the notice requirements to the candidates. The memorandum also addressed the recount process itself, including the programming of ballot tabulating equipment, notice requirements for county canvassing board meetings, procedures regarding observers, and a reminder that the recount was just that—a recount and not a recanvass of the entire election.

Finally, the memorandum reminded counties of the Secretary of State's Election Information Reporting System for reporting recount results, and provided contact information for the three gubernatorial candidates. State law required each county to notify all three candidates of the time and place of each county's recount, if it occurred.[24]

At the same time, two other 11th-hour issues surfaced that would impact the initial count and further stir the pot. Both worked to Gregoire's benefit.

First, King County announced it had dramatically underreported the number of ballots left to count. Election workers learned there were twice as many outstanding ballots—21,000, not the 11,000 previously announced.[25] While the number was an estimate, the dramatic increase raised speculation.

King County Elections Director Dean Logan attributed the wrong estimate to the surprising number of voters casting absentee and provisional ballots. This news was greeted with alarm by some Republican observers; 10,000 more ballots in King County, the Democratic stronghold, were immediately translated as a potential plus 2,000 votes for Gregoire.

The additional 10,000 ballots shocked those who had been predicted the likely outcome of the race based on King County's estimate. This revelation encouraged suspicions, especially on the blogs.

The additional votes became known as the "found ballots," when, in fact, no new ballots had been found at all. These ballots were in the possession of the county, or somewhere in the ballot-processing pipeline, all along.

A second bombshell occurred on November 15 when the Grays Harbor County Auditor notified the Secretary of State that a reporting error in its programming systems changed the vote totals by 508. Although Rossi previously had led the county by 231 votes, the error pushed Gregoire ahead by 277 votes.[26]

At the end of the day, November 15, Gregoire recaptured the lead by a thread—with a mere 158 votes.

Gregoire	1,360,871
Rossi	1,360,713
Bennett	62,439

County Auditors estimated 21,666 ballots yet to count, with two days left until final certification on November 17.

Secretary of State Retains Attorneys

By Tuesday, November 16, the effort by the Attorney General's Office to retain "independent" legal counsel for the Secretary of State moved into high gear.

Senior staff in the Attorney General's Office notified several Seattle law firms when looking for a balanced team of lawyers to represent the Secretary of State in future litigation regarding the Governor's race. Firms were invited to submit potential teams that offered experience in government representation, complex litigation, and election law. Any litigation team needed to be either politically neutral or have balanced representation for both political parties.

After reviewing several proposals, the Office of the Secretary of State advised the Attorney General's Office on November 16 that the Seattle law firm of Foster Pepper was the preferred choice. By 11a.m., November 16, the selected attorneys from Foster Pepper were appointed Special Assistant Attorneys General to represent the Secretary of State in any litigation regarding the Governor's race.

The Foster Pepper legal team consisted of Hugh Spitzer, Tom Ahearne, Jeff Richard, and Marco Magnano. Spitzer, a prominent Democrat, was well known for representing state and local agencies. Ahearne and Magnano were experienced in complex litigation. Richard, a prominent Republican, was the former Deputy Prosecuting Attorney for King County's Elections Department. As events developed, Ahearne became the chief litigator for the Secretary of State in the lawsuits that followed.

As early as the afternoon of November 16, just a few hours after his appointment as Special Assistant Attorney General, Ahearne observed Judge Lum's final rulings on provisional ballots from King County Superior Court.

November 17—The End of the Beginning

Wednesday, November 17—fifteen days after the election on November 2—was the statutory deadline for when all county canvassing boards certified the General Election returns.

Throughout the day, the counties tabulated the remaining ballots and completed the certification process. The results from small Columbia County were posted first on the Secretary of State Office's website (vote.wa.gov). Other county results continued to be posted throughout the day. People watched in fascination as the totals changed.

Finally, by 6:30 p.m., 38 of the 39 counties had reported final returns. The margin between the two candidates stood at a scant 13 votes. While the 13-vote margin favored Gregoire, the 39th county, Benton, was Rossi's biggest stronghold by percentage, a 70 to 30 advantage in favor of the Republican. Finally, at 6:33 p.m., Benton County completed its count and reported the numbers. Those anxiously waiting for the final results saw that Dino Rossi stood as the winner in the original count—by only a shocking 261 votes.

Rossi	1,371,414
Gregoire	1,371,153
Bennett	63,346

Rossi had prevailed by just 261 votes out of more than 2.8 million cast—a margin of 0.0093 percent. Rossi won 48.876 percent of the vote, while Gregoire received 48.867 percent.

This very close margin triggered a mandatory "machine" recount. The 2004 race for Governor was far from over.

Endnotes

1. KOMO Staff and News Services, "One Clear Winner: Turnout," KOMONews.com, November 1, 2004.
2. Office of the Secretary of State, "Reed Predicts Record Turnout," press release, October 19, 2004.
3. Susan Gilmore and Sara Jean Green, "Local Lawyers, Poll Observers Poised for Action," *Seattle Times*, October 28, 2004.
4. Neil Modie, "Parties Poised to Send Lawyers to State's Polls," *Post-Intelligencer*, October 30, 2004.
5. Associated Press, "Gregoire, Rossi in a Cliffhanger for Governor," *USA Today*, November 3, 2004.
6. Robert Mak, "The Longest Election Day," KING Television, Belo Corporation, November 21, 2004.
7. Ibid.
8. Rick Anderson and George Howland Jr., "Color Washington Purple," *Seattle Weekly*, November 3, 2004.
9. "Moving Forward after a Contentious Election," *Everett Herald*, November 3, 2004.
10. Nick Handy, email, November 3, 2004.
11. Angela Galloway, "Governor's Race Is So Close, No Winner Is Likely for Days," *Post-Intelligencer*, November 4, 2004.
12. Ralph Thomas, "Gregoire Edges Ahead of Rossi; Potential for Recount Looms," *Seattle Times*, November 4, 2004.
13. Ibid.
14. Office of the Secretary of State, email records, November 4, 2004.
15. Angela Galloway, "Rossi Edges into Slim Lead; More Votes Counted Today," *Post-Intelligencer*, November 10, 2004.
16. Ibid.
17. Angela Galloway, "Rossi Widens Lead but Race Stays Tight," *Post-Intelligencer*, November 11, 2004.
18. George Howland Jr., "Dinocracy in Action," *Seattle Weekly*, November 10, 2004.

19. Ralph Thomas, "Rossi Ahead, Names Team for Possible Transition," *Seattle Times*, November 10, 2004.
20. Angela Galloway, "Democrats Sue King County over Disputed Ballots," *Post-Intelligencer,* November 12, 2004.
21. Ibid.
22. Ibid.
23. Keith Ervin and Susan Gilmore, "Governor's Race: Judge Rules for Dems on Rejected Ballots," *Seattle Times*, November 12, 2004.
24. Nick Handy, "Procedures for Possible Recount in Gubernatorial Race," memorandum to county auditors from the Secretary of State Elections Division, November 15, 2004.
25. Dean Logan, email, November 15, 2004.
26. Vern Spatz, email, November 15, 2004.

If you aren't watching the Washington Governor's Election count—what's wrong with you?

Office of the Secretary of State

Chapter Four

The Media Whirlwind

By now, Washington's gubernatorial election had caught the attention of people who did not normally bother much with politics. Emotions ran the gamut. Many found the ongoing drama fascinating, while it infuriated others, such as Jay Carlson.

"The lack of a determination of the Governor's race at this late date is an embarrassment for this state...I believe this is the last race in the United States for which the initial vote count is not yet known. We voted on November 2. Today is November 17!"[1]

Carlson was correct. According to the *Los Angeles Times*, Washington's gubernatorial election was, in fact, the country's last undecided race of 2004.[2]

By November 17, election mistakes and nonstop media attention had resulted in an uproar from the public, and an exhausting schedule for the political campaigns and the Secretary of State elections staff, and also consumed the attention and time of elections people in the 39 counties. Reporters from the state and national media were calling at all hours and without warning.

On November 17, the media crowds into a Secretary of State's office building for a live press conference. That same day, the staff moved the office back to the recently renovated Capitol Building, marking one of the busiest days of the year.
Office of the Secretary of State

Meanwhile, the Secretary of State's crisis team had decided that continuous updates for the public were a top priority. On this mid-November day when the counties "certified" results, Reed had begun with commuter-time radio interviews at 6:30 a.m. and continued with others throughout the day. He also held a live televised press conference in the late afternoon, and did not finish his last conversation with a reporter until 11 p.m.

During the afternoon press conference, all attention focused on the election. "Sam Reed has just stepped to the microphone right now to give us the word," Rich Johnson relayed live to KIRO Radio listeners.[3]

The *New York Times* noted: "At a televised news conference in Olympia, the state capital, the secretary of state, Sam Reed, could barely contain a laugh when at 4:30 p.m. he announced the latest results."[4] (Two more hours remained before the last counties "certified.")

"The race for Governor in the state of Washington in 2004 is unprecedented," said Reed in a strained but steady voice. "At this minute, Attorney General Gregoire has a 34-vote lead. But some of the counties that have yet to come in are Benton, Clark, Franklin, Skamania, all of which carried for Senator Rossi, and Grays Harbor, which has split pretty closely and they're counting absentees. So, it looks like it's going to be within a few hundred votes. So later today I will be calling for a recount."[5]

The Law on Recounts

What triggers a recount in Washington State? A gap in the number of votes cast for candidates, or in support of, or against, a State measure, must be less than .5 percent or fewer than 2,000 votes. Since 1968, six races—involving both ballot measures and candidates—have triggered a mandatory statewide recount. Numerous other races, including elections for the U.S. Congress, also have required a mandatory recount (RCW 29A.64.021)

Mandatory recounts were required in the 2000 U.S. Senate race between challenger Maria Cantwell (D) and incumbent Slade Gorton (R), and also the Secretary of State election between former Congressman Don Bonker (D) and then-Thurston County Auditor Sam Reed (R). Although media coverage was extensive, the other close election that year—between George Bush and Al Gore—garnered most of the headlines nationally, and dominated the news in Washington State. The Cantwell-Gorton race was extremely important, as ultimately the control of the U.S. Senate rested on the outcome.

The initial certification of that election showed 1,199,260 votes for Cantwell and 1,197,307 for Gorton, with a margin of 1,953 votes for Cantwell. The subsequent machine recount gave Cantwell 1,199,437 votes and Gorton 1,197,208, thereby increasing Cantwell's margin by 2,229. Gorton did not request a manual recount following the machine count. In the 2000 election, Cantwell won only five counties—Jefferson, King, San Juan, Snohomish, and Thurston.

That evening, in an act normally billed as little more than a formality, Reed completed the partial canvass of the General Election returns, officially certifying the 261 vote difference between the top two gubernatorial candidates, giving Rossi the advantage.

Reporter Rich Johnson broke the news on KIRO Radio. "What we do know from talk around the office is that the Benton County 750 final votes have given Dino Rossi a final lead of 261 votes. That's Rossi—261 over Gregoire."[6]

The slight margin of victory was historic, and narrow enough to trigger a mandatory "machine" recount under State law. The order from Secretary Reed read as follows: "I further certify that the difference (261) between the number of votes cast for the two top candidates for this office (Christine Gregoire and Dino Rossi) is less than one-half of one percent of the total vote cast for these two candidates and less than 2,000 votes. Therefore, pursuant to RCW 29A.64.020, I hereby order that a machine recount be made of all votes cast for the Office of Governor of the State of Washington and the county canvassing boards of the counties involved certify the results of said recount to the Secretary of State in the manner provided by RCW 29A.64.040."[7]

Reed noted it was a defining moment in Washington State politics. "We're making history, not the kind of history I thought we'd be making on November 2nd, but history nonetheless."[8]

As Reed pointed out to the *Post-Intelligencer*, had the margin of victory been even narrower a "manual" recount would have been required, which could be incredibly grueling. A hand count "is the toughest kind of election to administer you can imagine," he said. "We've all seen human errors, and we've seen it in this election. But when you're doing this manually, it is common practice to have mistakes…I hope this election will send a clear message to the citizens of the state just how important voting is."[9]

The machine recount order certainly sent a message to the main and alternative media that the Rossi-Gregoire election was shaping up to be one of the year's most sensational national stories.

Word of the recount inspired the following message on Murdoc Online out of Grand Rapids, Michigan: "If you aren't watching the Washington Governor's Election count—what's wrong with you?

"Now that this preliminary nonsense is over, the recount, lawsuits, and conspiracy theories can finally begin… good night."[10]

November 18

The next morning, news of the recount was delivered with the morning newspapers.

> **"Rossi Holds 261-vote Lead over Gregoire"** declared Vancouver's *Columbian.*[11]

Thurston County Recounts

Before assuming duties as Secretary of State, Sam Reed served five terms as Thurston County Auditor. Like many county auditors across the state, Reed acquired considerable experience administering recounts and close contests (see below).

Election	Race	Candidates	Votes Cast	First Results	Votes Cast	Recount Results
11/2000	US Senator	Maria Cantwell	50410	52.25	50436	52.26
		Slade Gorton	42796	44.36	42804	44.36
		Jeff Jared	3264	3.38	3263	3.38
11/2000	Secretary of State	Sam Reed	54672	59.21	54692	59.20
		Don Bonker	32753	35.47	32765	35.47
		J. Bradley Gibson	3059	3.31	3064	3.32
		Chris Loftis	1858	2.01	1858	2.01
9/2000	Legislative Dist 35	Kathy Haigh	2684	57.46	2685	57.45
	Position 1	Wendy Ervin	867	18.56	867	18.55
		Frank Dare	852	18.24	854	18.27
		Marti Lewis	268	5.74	268	5.73
9/1999	Lacey City Council	Mary Dean	2272	42.82	2272	42.82
	Position 3	Randy Brooks	1521	28.67	1521	28.67
		Kathleen Rooney	1513	28.51	1513	28.51
11/1999	Position 7	Chris Parsons	1831	50.25	1831	50.25
	Tumwater City Council	John Brown	1813	49.75	1813	49.75
11/1996	US Representative	Brian Baird	29585	56.79	29579	56.78
	District 3	Linda Smith	22514	43.21	22512	43.22
11/1990	Low Income Housing	No	24719	51.19	24721	51.19
	SJR 8212	Yes	23574	48.81	23576	48.81
11/1989	Fire District 12	Robert Rose	212	50.00	212	50.00
	Position 2	Oscar Kosola	212	50.00	212	50.00
11/1989	Freeholder Dist. 2	Randy Scott	5619	21.42	5621	21.43
	Position 9	Teresa Jennings	5583	21.29	5585	21.29
		Bill Pilkey	4783	18.24	4783	18.23
		Alan Corwin	3528	13.45	3528	13.45
		Ed Kenney	3500	13.34	3500	13.34
		T L Green-Huntamer	3216	12.26	3216	12.26
11/1988	US Representative	Jolene Unsoeld	34839	53.25	34842	53.25
	District 3	Bill Wight	30589	46.75	30594	46.75
11/1984	Legislative Dist 20	Stuart Halsan	7533	53.65	7536	53.65
		W H Fuller	6507	46.35	6510	46.35

Meanwhile, the sequence of events triggered by the recount order began. Most important was notifying the candidates by certified mail, informing them of the date and time that the machine recount would begin in each county. Reed also made personal phone calls to the candidates. Most hoped the recount would be completed before the Thanksgiving holiday.

November 19

While the counties prepared for the recount, the political parties positioned themselves for battle. Rumors circulated that the Democrats already were considering a second recount—this one by hand—of the 2.8 million ballots.

A "recount is likely," said Democratic Party Chair Paul Berendt. "It's very likely we'll get through the mechanical recount and then go right into a hand recount—if not the whole state, at least individual counties that we think warrant a closer look."[12]

The Republicans issued a warning of their own. "We're going to have observers everywhere, and we're not going to hesitate to go to court if we think there's something going wrong," noted Chairman Chris Vance. Regarding a possible manual recount, Vance replied that it was a matter of "crossing that bridge when we come to it." He added: "We are prepared to do anything and everything necessary to protect our interest in this."[13]

As Secretary Reed made clear, whatever the result of the machine recount, the State could not order and pay for a second (manual) recount. No provision existed in law for the State to fund anything but a single, mandatory recount. However, State law did allow for either political party to request a second recount providing the party footed the bill.

If the race remained extremely close in the machine count, of course, a second recount was likely. If the margin ended in "30 to 40 votes, then it would make a lot of sense for them to want to recount again," Reed said.[14]

That evening, Sheryl Moss of the Office of the Secretary of State received a call from election staff in Pacific and Kittitas counties, stating they discovered ballots not included in their original canvass. Moss reported: "Pacific found one ballot in a group of empty absentee envelopes. Kittitas discovered 33 ballots, approved by the Canvassing Board, but not duplicated or counted. They have both been instructed to document the reasons, explain it to their observers when the recount is conducted, and include the ballots in the recount."[15]

November 20

The next day the political firestorm intensified. KIRO News Radio said it was "just getting word that state Republicans are very angry and upset with how King County is storing some

The Secretary of State's recount team for the 2004 Governor's race—(l. to r.) Trova Heffernan, Pam Floyd, John Pearson, Sam Reed, Steve Excell, Nick Handy, Joanie Deutsch, and Shane Hamlin. *Washington State Senate*

ballots ahead of tomorrow's recount for the Governor's Election."[16]

"The problem is there are hundreds and hundreds of blank ballots sitting in there unsecured in shallow mailing trays. Nobody knows exactly how many there are," commented the Republicans' Vance. "They could easily be taken out, altered, and added to the stream of ballots."[17]

Dean Logan, manager of King County Elections, and previously an Elections Director for Secretary of State Sam Reed, defended the county's procedures. Logan explained that marked ballots were kept securely inside sealed containers and guarded around the clock by uniformed deputies.[18]

Meanwhile the Democrats responded to Chairman Vance, saying if he was "really concerned about the potential of fraud, he should go ahead and ask for the manual recount now, or call on the Secretary of State to order one."[19]

Of course, the Secretary of State had no authority to order a manual recount.

"We're going to make sure, in this recount, every single vote counts," Gregoire vowed. "This is not about Republican or Democrat, Libertarian or Independent, this is about all of us as Washingtonians, standing up, casting our ballots."[20]

The Count Begins; Republican Party Sues King County and Sam Reed

To effectively communicate internally, the Office of the Secretary of State established a war room in its Elections Division, which included a team of decision makers from the executive staff as well as Secretary Reed, Assistant Secretary Steve Excell, Communications Director Trova Heffernan, and Communications Manager Joanie Deutsch. For months, this group would be at ground zero in the controversial recount.

Reed spent the bulk of his time as the chief agency spokesperson—handling media interviews, participating in and leading briefings, and making strategic decisions. Communication between the war room and the executive staff proved critical in ensuring that a consistent, accurate message was provided to the public.

The war room, set up at the Elections Division headquarters down the street from the Capitol Building, looked the part of a command central. The room was typically littered with pizza boxes, chip bags, bottled water, and soda containers. The war room dealt with many policy decisions, media interviews, and walk-in visitors, and also regularly dispatched staff to various counties when the need arose. Elections Director Nick Handy and Deputy Elections Director John Pearson alerted the agency's crisis team about details occurring in the counties, including media calls.

The first day of the historic machine recount fell on Saturday, November 20. Within a matter of hours, the Republican Party filed a lawsuit in U.S. District Court. The party—concerned, of course, that the recount in the Seattle area might benefit Gregoire—sought a temporary restraining order to stop King County from reviewing ballots by hand that the machines had rejected.

Representing the Secretary of State, Attorney Tom Ahearne received the Republicans' pleadings by email.

> Dear Tom:
>
> Please find attached papers and pleadings for a lawsuit and motion for temporary restraining order against the Secretary of State. I understand that another representative of my clients has either reached you or is trying to reach you to arrange service. I also understand that a judge has been arranged for 5pm and that we will be asking for a prompt hearing on the motion.
>
> Robert Maguire
>
> Davis Wright Tremaine LLP[21]

In their pleadings, Republican Party lawyers argued that the plaintiffs were being "irreparably harmed by King County's unconstitutional recount procedure. Because original ballots are being enhanced on the basis of a subjective determination of voter 'intent,' each 'enhancement' is final and cannot be reviewed or re-examined. Moreover, such ballots would be difficult, if not impossible to locate, as King County

Understanding Ballot Enhancement

In teams of two and under supervision, election workers are allowed to "enhance" ballots under State law.

This enhancement process allows the machines to properly interpret the voter's intent and count the ballots correctly. For example, if a voter circled ovals instead of filling them in as would be proper, an election worker fills in the same ovals the voter circled. The voter's original marks remain visible on the ballot. The voting equipment then reads this "enhanced" ballot.

Understanding Ballot Duplication

Ballot "duplication" means that the original ballot is duplicated to a new ballot. This is done by duplication boards, consisting of two election staff members working under close supervision and in the presence of political party observers. The duplication board marks a new ballot consistent with the voter's marks from the original ballot, which could not be read by a tabulating machine. A new ballot is prepared for the tabulating machine that is consistent with the voter's original intent. The original ballot is kept secure, and identifying information is marked on both ballots recording the transaction.

is simply mixing them back into the general ballot pool once the 'enhancement' is complete. In other words, once enhanced, an egg cannot be unscrambled; and as each hour passes, more and more eggs are broken."[22]

In essence, according to the party, the recount should only include ballots tallied in the original November 2 count.

But State law did not allow for such a policy. Washington was a voter-intent state. If the intent of the voter was clear, the ballot must be counted—even if the voter failed to follow instructions by, for example, circling an oval instead of filling it in, which automatic machines could not read.

To determine voter intent while preserving voters' original marks on their ballots, election workers could enhance or duplicate ballots under State law. The enhancement and duplication of ballots allowed for the ballots to then be counted properly by a machine.

November 21

Meanwhile, U.S. District Court Judge Marsha Pechman, during a Sunday conference call, denied the Republican request for a court order to stop the enhancement process. Judge Pechman said there was no need to disrupt the process since the ballots were not being destroyed and could be reviewed later.

As the recount proceeded, the Office of the Secretary of State and the county auditors began receiving their fair share of visitors and calls from interested parties. The Elections Division heard regularly from Democrat attorneys Jenny Durkan, Kevin Hamilton, and David Burman, either by telephone, email, or letter. Peter Schalestock, a Republican Party staff attorney, was in contact with Assistant Secretary Steve Excell.

These initial contacts concerned basic procedural issues in the recount. On occasion, the parties requested that the Secretary of State play a more active role, correcting what they claimed were county auditors' errors or discrepancies. The Elections Division's typical response was to gather the underlying facts, consult with county auditors, resolve the issues, and advise all parties concerned about the final outcome. Sometimes, this involved dispatching Elections Division staff to assist a particular county auditor.

November 22

Indeed, as the counties continued to recount the ballots, problems emerged. On November 22, Elections Director Nick Handy alerted the staff by email. "Ferry County's recount did not come out well and we have asked them to break it down by precinct and try to solve the problem. We are rerouting Paul Miller who has been at Yakima and Benton today to head up to Ferry."[23]

In Snohomish County, an election worker discovered 224 properly marked but uncounted ballots sitting in a tray in a secured room. The ballots had been prepared for counting, but mistakenly placed in a stack of empty trays. When additional trays were added, the ballots were buried out of sight.

After finding the ballots, Snohomish County Auditor Bob Terwilliger immediately reported the situation to the county canvassing board. The board determined that an inadvertent mistake was made, that the ballots were missed during the original count, and that security had been maintained on the ballots at all times. Accordingly, the board directed that the votes be counted.

Despite the newly added votes, the county's recount of more than 350,000 ballots only resulted in a net change of one vote, due to the fact that Snohomish County voted fairly evenly between Gregoire and Rossi.

The Recount and Back to Federal Court Again

By the end of the day, November 22, the machine recount was completed in 24 counties. Most of these results favored Rossi, adding some 25 votes to his original 261 vote lead. King County, however, was not scheduled to complete its recount until November 24. King County, of course, included one-third of the state's voters and heavily favored Gregoire. Nevertheless, so far in the county Rossi had added 85 votes and Gregoire 60, for a net gain of 25 votes for Rossi. As more ballots from the original count were processed, election workers continued to review problematical ballots to learn voters' intent.

On this same day, the Republicans again attempted to obtain a federal court order to stop the recount. They expressed concerns over the enhancement and duplication process, and claimed that the counties had different standards for processing ballots initially rejected by the tabulating machines.

"Applying counting standards in selected counties different from those in others violates the equal protection and due process protections of the U.S. and Washington constitutions and ultimately will deny Washington voters... their fundamental right to vote," the lawsuit stated.

State Elections Director Nick Handy replied that he had not seen anything wrong with how King County or other counties were handling the ballots. "We are very comfortable with the duplication and enhancement process," Handy said. "We're comfortable that the counties are doing this consistently."[24]

U.S. District Court Judge Ricardo Martinez denied the Republicans' request, and set a November 30 hearing date—two days before the State deadline to certify the results.

November 23

On this day, Cowlitz County reported that fewer ballots and fewer votes were counted in the recount than during the original count. This gave rise to the specter of "lost ballots." The Elections Division dispatched Paul Miller to Cowlitz County to review the situation. After a thorough review, Miller and County Auditor Kris Swanson determined that an identified group of absentee ballots was inadvertently counted twice on election night.

Handy sent the following email to Secretary Reed and Assistant Secretary Excell:

"Cowlitz just called to advise they recounted 99 fewer ballots in the recount. Kris Swanson's explanation is that the operator error in the original count most likely resulted in some ballots being counted more than once. Thus, Cowlitz will report 29 fewer votes for Gregoire and 40 fewer votes for Rossi. The bottom line is a net gain to Gregoire of 11 votes."[25]

By the evening of November 23, all but two counties had reported their recount results.[26] Rossi now stood 321 votes ahead of Gregoire. Only King and Whitman counties had yet to report their recount results. Once more, the state party chairs weighed in. The Democratic Party sent out a news release announcing ballot counting discrepancies and errors throughout the state. A hand recount, the party insisted, seemed to be the only way to ensure accuracy.

The Role of the Secretary of State

The Office of the Secretary of State worked closely with the county auditors to resolve any discrepancies. Meanwhile, advocates for the candidates were contacting the Secretary of State's Office demanding that more be done than just investigating and conferring with county auditors—they wanted active intervention by the Secretary in the recount process itself. These requests revealed a widespread misunderstanding about the Secretary of State's role in elections.

The misperception was that the Secretary of State maintains regulatory power over decisions in the counties—this is what prompted the requests and demands that the Secretary overrule a county decision. Quite simply, the Secretary lacked this authority for historical reasons.

Framers of the Constitution

In 1889, Washington's constitutional framers wanted the people (voters) to retain as much control of government as possible. Consequently, the constitutional delegates were a distrustful bunch when it came to granting and dispensing power. Thus, Washington State's new government divided executive power by having nine statewide elected offices (a number of states elect fewer statewide officials), and the Washington Constitution also called for the election of all nine members of the State Supreme Court (many states allow the governor to appoint judges).

Similarly, the constitutional framers wanted as much local control as possible over State voting, resulting in the delegation of power to counties in elections. Final authority rested in each county's canvassing board, not the Secretary of State. While the Secretary of State was authorized to implement laws and ensure consistency through rules and standards, key decisions during and after an election resided at the county level.

Over the years, the Elections Division had evolved into playing a collaborative role with the counties, but the Secretary of State did not have the authority to overrule or invalidate decisions made by county auditors or canvassing boards.

When Rossi or Gregoire advocates now began requesting or demanding action by the Secretary of State, a Washington State civics lesson usually resulted, explaining that the recount—like the rest of the election—was a process involving a number of key players in different roles, including the county auditors, the county canvassing boards, and the Office of the Secretary of State. This message was a difficult sell and one typically not happily received; most of the candidates' proponents were seeking a command and control effort by the Secretary of State that simply was unauthorized by law. The Secretary did not have the statutory authority to correct errors on the part of the counties.

Each county canvassing board retained authority to correct discrepancies or errors presented by the county auditor, but only until the returns were certified. After certification, legal action was required to make further changes.

These explanations were rarely popular with the political parties or engaged citizens, who deluged the Secretary of State's Office with concerns, complaints, and suggestions regarding alleged errors. Not surprisingly, those supporting Rossi tended to express concerns about King County, a Gregoire stronghold. Gregoire supporters, on the other hand, were more focused on alleged mistakes in Adams, Grant, Franklin, and other pro-Rossi counties.

November 24

When King County posted results on Wednesday, November 24, the State had concluded its machine recount. The numbers were staggering.

"I have been in this business for 33 years and I am astonished," Sam Reed told a crowd of reporters during a live televised press conference. "In fact, when they gave me these results, I must admit…I was stunned."[27]

As is often the case in recounts, almost all of the counties had added votes to their totals. Christine Gregoire picked up 1,289 votes, Dino Rossi added 1,070 votes, and Ruth Bennett increased her support by 54 votes.

Rossi	1,372,484
Gregoire	1,372,442
Bennett	63,415

Rossi and Gregoire had split the electorate in half. After two counts of 2.8 million ballots, the candidates stood only a remarkable 42 votes apart. Rossi had carried 32 counties, and Gregoire 7.

To the elections administrators, a 42 vote difference out of more than 2.8 million ballots was the kind of unbelievable, historic event that they wish had not occurred. Reed would famously say that election workers do not particularly care who wins—only that a victor wins "big" with a large margin, which eliminates any controversy over vote counts.

"On November 30th, Governor Gary Locke and I will certify this election and certify that Dino Rossi was elected Governor of the State of Washington," explained Reed. "At the conclusion of that certification, I will open up a three-day filing period during which either of the political parties or the candidates could file for a recount."[28]

Reed assumed at this point that a candidate or political party would request a "manual" recount. In his experience, he knew that political parties tended to call for a recount in those portions of the state creating the best possibilities for their candidate.

If this occurred, "then by state law I am required to then call for another recount of all other counties in the state of Washington to be done in the same manner."[29] Reed would then issue an order on Monday, December 6, giving the counties a two-day notice. (For King County, Washington's most populous county, this kind of tedious, detail-driven process would take longest—10 days.)

"It really is what you saw in Florida, holding up the ballot and seeing if the 'chad' has fallen out," he said.[30]

Reed outlined several lessons revealed by the stunning turn of events following the November 2 count.

- Showed the importance of every vote.
- Demonstrated the need to re-examine our election process that was designed when mail balloting was rare. (In the 2004 Governor's race, more than 68 percent of voters cast ballots by mail.)
- It opened election administrators' eyes—and the public's for that matter—to the King County ruling on provisional ballots.

"And I must say I was disturbed at the thought of the political parties going out and going to people's homes asking what party they are and then if they're the right party then getting the signature to get their ballot counted," said Reed. "That is wrong."[31]

Reed also cautioned reporters about the emotions involved in a high-profile recount of this magnitude: "Every error is blown up, becomes controversial and is news.

"As we get into a manual recount, you're going to hear some real questions raised because that is part of what the party observers are doing. I urge you to recognize that the political parties' role is not to be the objective election administrators who want a free and fair and open election. Their role is to help their candidate win."

A question was raised about election worker mistakes.

"I would like to see them not make any mistakes," replied Reed. "But, having been in the front lines, I can tell you with all the pressure that's on you, the hours that you're working, the fatigue that sets in...the number of people that are coming at you all of the time and the demands on you, that human beings are going to make errors. And I haven't seen anything that I view as anything other than an honest human mistake that is correctable."[32]

Why Votes Change in a Recount

Questions naturally emerged regarding how votes could be added during a recount when new votes were not allowed. In some instances, allegations were made that "new" ballots had been added to the count. With the exception of a handful of misplaced ballots found during the recount, this was simply not the case.

In almost every instance, the added votes were not from new ballots. Rather, votes that were cast on General Election day were added following a closer inspection of these ballots as they circulated through the recount process. This would prove especially true in counties using precinct-based ballot counters. In those counties, including King, Pierce, and Spokane, a number of votes were detected to now be valid by a visual examination during the recount. This inspection was not possible during the original count because these ballots had been fed directly into the ballot tabulating equipment by the voter in a polling place. Thus, the recount offered the first opportunity for a visual inspection of these ballots by an election official.

Although the ballot-counting machines used in precincts were programmed to reject completely blank ballots, tabulators were not able to detect voter intent when, perhaps, the wrong mark was made only for the office of Governor, or where the voter had not otherwise marked a ballot properly.

The Secretary of State's Office had adopted administrative rules following the 2000 Presidential election to offer consistent guidance to county auditors on "what is a vote." Following the U.S. Supreme Court's decision in *Bush v. Gore*, whatever constituted a valid vote in one county must also constitute a valid vote in every other county. In Washington, those standards were in place.

After inspection afforded by a machine recount, King County added 971 votes, Pierce County 514 , and Spokane County 261.[33] For the most part, these were votes that would have been considered either as overvotes (voting for more than one candidate) or undervotes (voting for neither candidate) during the original count. In each instance, visual inspection allowed human eyes to detect what the machine could not.

Vote totals changed for other reasons, too, mostly relating to human error. As mentioned earlier, Cowlitz County showed fewer ballots than during the initial count; the final determination was that a group of ballots was inadvertently processed twice during the original count. In Snohomish County, a misplaced tray of 224 ballots not tabulated during the original count was discovered during the recount process. After the Snohomish County Canvassing Board determined these ballots were maintained in secure storage during the intervening period, they were included in the recount. A similar situation occurred in Kittitas County with 34 ballots, resolved in a similar manner. With the exception of Cowlitz County, each of these situations, and almost all others, resulted in counties adding votes during the mandatory recount.

Nick Handy, the Director of Elections, explained that in a recount anomalies generally occur in the same proportion as the original count of ballots. "That's what happens in a recount. It's rare that you have a situation that has a disproportionate benefit to one of the candidates."[34]

The Reaction

The news media from all across the nation ran the story.

> **"Rossi Wins Recount for Governor Seat"** headlined the *Beacon Journal* in Akron, Ohio.[35]

> **"GOP Hopeful Gets 42-vote Edge in Washington Governor's Race"** declared Georgia's *Augusta Chronicle*.[36]

The candidates and their campaigns reached predictable conclusions.

"Well, the race continues," noted Gregoire on KIRO Radio. "With nearly three million votes cast there is a 42-vote difference. My friends, it is a tied race."[37]

"Dino Rossi is the governor-elect," Republican Chairman Chris Vance said strongly. "He won the election. He won the recount. It is certainly close. But I hope Christine Gregoire will take a few days and do the right thing for the state of Washington and concede the election."[38]

As a result of Gregoire's claim of a "tied race," a Rossi blogger published a spoof announcing that the Seattle Seahawks had tied the Dallas Cowboys 41–39 in the previous Monday night football game.

November 30

By 11 a.m. on November 30, the wild political drama promised more uncertainty as Secretary Reed prepared to certify the machine recount and open the door to yet another recount.

"Welcome to what is truly an historic certification of election results," Reed said to reporters. "We have checked with experts around the nation and nowhere has there ever been an election of this magnitude that is this close."[39]

Reed's office also issued a media advisory:

"Olympia…Following a mandatory, machine recount in an historic race for Governor, Secretary of State Sam Reed today certified the 2004 General Election. Republican Dino Rossi prevailed with a 42-vote lead over Democrat Christine Gregoire. A recount is almost a certainty. The candidates and political parties have until 5 p.m. Friday, December 3, to request and pay for an additional recount. The cost is 25 cents a ballot in a hand recount and 15 cents a ballot in a machine recount."[40]

Reed explained that following certification, the candidates, campaigns, or parties would have three business days to request a full or partial hand recount at their own expense. Should a hand recount request be received, it would begin Monday, December 6. The Secretary advised that a statewide hand recount would take approximately two weeks.

Reed also noted that a manual recount was an expensive, labor-intensive proposition.

"I'd be comfortable with calling the race over right now. But I also believe that it is the right of these candidates and the parties to do it, and I don't question them for exercising their right. When you're behind you want to exhaust every opportunity you have to win the race."[41]

He also recognized that the Democrats accused him of rushing certification.

"We are confident that the counties had solved their problems, otherwise we would not proceed. I would not sign these papers today if that were not the case."[42]

The Recall Attempt of Sam Reed

The turmoil surrounding the Governor's race prompted some citizens to take matters into their own hands and initiate a recall effort against the Secretary of State. Apparently, Sam Reed is the only Washington Secretary of State in history to face a recall attempt—in fact, there were two recall filings. On January 14, 2005, citizen Martin Ringhofer filed charges, accusing the Secretary of failing to perform his duties.

Websites and blogs (such as www.recallreed.blogspot.com, which is no longer available) promoted the effort by attempting to play on the emotions of disappointed voters and rallying support to remove Reed from office.

From the moment the charges were filed, the Attorney General's Office advised Reed that the accusations lacked real merit and appeared more as an emotional reaction to the disputed election. Ringhofer's initial charges failed to satisfy the basic requirements of the statutes. Ringhofer not only failed to sign the charges under oath, he did not sign them at all.

State law requires that recall charges must demonstrate malfeasance, misfeasance, or a violation of the oath of office. For the purposes of a recall, the law defines malfeasance or misfeasance as "wrongful conduct that affects, interrupts, or interferes, with the performance of official duty." A violation of the oath of office is defined as "willful neglect or failure by an elective public officer to perform faithfully a duty imposed by law." An elected official cannot be recalled for making an unpopular decision, or for using discretion allowed to him under law. When a recall petition is filed, it is reviewed and processed by the Attorney General's Office. A court of law must then decide whether the allegations meet the criteria, and if a recall may be pursued.

Even before the court dismissed the initial charges, Ringhofer and recall partner Linda Jordan filed a second statement of charges. The number of charges was expanded, supplemental material provided, and the charges were signed under oath.

Ringhofer and Jordan held Reed accountable for voting irregularities in King County—the first six charges made against the Secretary fell into this category. During the 2004 election, however, Reed had no authority over any county. It was not permissible under law, for example, to make command or personnel decisions of any kind. The first six charges, therefore, were found factually insufficient because they did not allege misconduct by the Secretary or his staff. Instead, they alleged misconduct by King County.

Ringhofer and Jordan also accused the Secretary of accepting an incomplete abstract of votes from 24 counties. The court found this charge factually and legally insufficient because it included "no specific allegation regarding knowledge by Reed." In addition, the court found "no evidence the irregularities were substantial enough to have made a difference in actions taken by Reed."

In the eighth charge—failing to adopt and enforce consistent standards in various counties across the state—the court acknowledged that even Ringhofer and Jordan recognized Reed set and implemented standards. They were really accusing him of failing to enforce them. Judge Wickham, however, found the charge legally insufficient because there was no evidence of misfeasance, malfeasance, or a violation of Reed's oath of office.

Finally, Ringhofer and Jordan accused Reed of certifying results of the final count despite his knowledge of voting irregularities. The court concluded that certification was either ministerial or involved some kind of discretion on the part of the Secretary. If the Secretary used discretion, he was required to determine the significance of a voting irregularity, whether it could be corrected, and the result of disenfranchising legal voters if he refused to certify results. According to Judge Wickham, no facts were alleged to show the Secretary's "exercise of discretion involved fraud or was arbitrary"—the criteria clearly established by the court. The judge found this last charge legally insufficient.

On February 7, 2005, Judge Wickham entered an order dismissing all charges as legally and/or factually insufficient. Ringhofer and Jordan appealed directly to the State Supreme Court. This court affirmed Wickham's order on December 1, 2005.

The Democrats were clearly preparing for another recount of the ballots. Governor Gary Locke pointed out that Rossi won the second mechanical count by just 42 votes, and that a manual recount was the only way to resolve the election with certainty.[43] Reed said that although he had confidence the recount was accurate, human error and ballot changes caused by handling likely meant that a hand count would provide a third result.[44]

Democratic Party spokeswoman Kristin Brost said: "There's a long list of counties where ballot numbers don't match up—where ballots either materialized or ballots evaporated. There may be perfectly reasonable explanations, but it needs to be explored."[45]

The Democrats indicated a preference for a complete hand recount, but expressed concern whether they could come up with sufficient funds to pay for it. (It would cost an estimated $730,000 to conduct a full, statewide recount, and the money had to be raised by the deadline imposed by law.)[46]

Not surprisingly, Rossi saw no need for a third count of the ballots. "We were certified. We won the recount with 42 votes. And we need to move forward now."[47] Rossi claimed that a hand recount would be less accurate than a machine recount. "If you count and recount and recount and keep counting until you finally win, what do you really have at the end?" he asked. "More of an illegitimate governorship."[48]

Meanwhile the state's newspapers began to weigh in on the second recount and questions of fraud. Accusations of cheating had been advanced by Internet bloggers directly, and also were implied by some of the major figures in the election.

Seattle's *Post-Intelligencer* left no doubt where it stood on the requested recount and the possibility that the Democrats, citing a lack of money, might only select certain counties for a manual count.

"Baloney," it editorialized. "The two parties spent more than $11 million on this race. There's no question it's worth spending another $730,000—the estimated cost of a statewide hand recount—in a last ditch effort to win it."[49]

"If state and national Democratic officials want to retain a Democratic governorship in Washington State, they can find the money."[50]

The newspaper was particularly critical of the idea that the party might "cherry-pick" counties to glean votes. "Presuming Gregoire could win ultimately, she still must be able to govern...if the lead changes in Gregoire's favor it would merely trigger a taxpayer-funded hand recount in all the other counties. That likely would leave a bad taste in the mouths of many voters. Worse, it could lend unwarranted gravitas to so-far scurrilous allegations of a 'stolen' election."[51]

The *Seattle Times* was no less insistent that any requested hand recount must be statewide. "It's easy to understand the idea of trying to save money and recount specific precincts where Democrat Gregoire is likely to pick up votes—or Republican Rossi is likely to lose them," they editorialized.[52]

"Logical? Yes. Strategic? Yes. But that is not the way to avoid long-term resentment over vote counting. Washington residents and both candidates have to live with the results of this election a long time. Gregoire cannot behave as if she wants vote counting to continue until she wins. The closer the state gets to a reliable count, the better."[53]

Peter Callaghan, a columnist for Tacoma's *News Tribune*, took issue with the allegations of election fraud emerging from the blogs and now entering the mainstream media. After noting that "irregularities" had been discovered during the recount, he commented:

"What, you might wonder, is a voting irregularity? As defined by the chairman of the state Democratic and Republican parties, it is anything that favors the other candidate. When they say 'voting irregularity' they want us to hear 'voter fraud.'"

"Maybe," he went on to say, "it is too much to ask for political parties and political campaigns to be dispassionate. They are all about winning, and we probably shouldn't expect them to lose gracefully for the good of the state and its residents.

"Someone, however, should point out that we're not Florida. The counts and recounts have proved that the vote-counting system in Washington is working as it was intended to work and is working pretty well—especially given the closeness of the vote.

"We have an election where the difference between the top two candidates is the equivalent of a tossed coin landing on its edge."[54]

Former Governor Dan Evans, a Rossi supporter, was outspoken in his belief that enough was enough. Although he assumed incorrectly that the Democrats would only ask for a partial recount, his conclusion about court involvement would prove all too accurate.

"We are getting to the point where the Gregoire campaign wants to pick and choose the areas where they count," he said. "They are not interested in an accurate count; they are interested in some combination of circumstances that might put their candidate ahead...

"I'm really concerned about that. I think we're headed down a long, devious, and uncontrolled path. Everybody seems to think a hand count is the ultimate in accuracy, and I don't think that's even remotely close to the truth...it's going to be interpretation. It's going to be lawyers. It's going to be the courts. I don't want this election to be settled by lawyers and the courts. We had enough of that four years ago."[55]

Endnotes

1. Jay Carlson, email, November 17, 2004.
2. "Washington Governor's Race Remains Undecided," *Los Angeles Times*, November 6, 2004.
3. Rich Johnson, 2004 election coverage, KIRO 710 Newsradio, Bonneville International Corporation, November 17, 2004.
4. Sarah Kershaw, "Official Orders Recount in Washington State," *New York Times*, November 18, 2004.
5. Office of the Secretary of State, "Reed Orders Recount in Governor's Race," press conference, November 17, 2004.
6. Rich Johnson, 2004 election coverage, KIRO 710 Newsradio, Bonneville International Corporation, November 17, 2004.
7. "Report of the Partial Canvass of the Returns of the State General Election Held on November 2, 2004," November 17, 2004.
8. Office of the Secretary of State, "Reed Orders Machine Recount in Governor's Race," press conference, November 17, 2004.
9. Angela Galloway, et al., "It's Rossi, by 0.0093," *Post-Intelligencer*, November 18, 2004.
10. Shelby Murdoc, comment on Murdoc Online Master Archives, www.murdoconline.net/archives.html, posted November 17, 2004.
11. Rebecca Cook (for the Associated Press), *Columbian*, November 18, 2004.
12. Angela Galloway, "State Gets Ready for Recount," *Post-Intelligencer*, November 19, 2004.
13. Ibid.

14. Ibid.
15. Sheryl Moss, email, November 19, 2004.
16. 2004 election coverage, KIRO 710 Newsradio, Bonneville International Corporation, November 20, 2004.
17. Ibid.
18. Christine Frey, "GOP Worries about Ballot Security," *Post-Intelligencer*, November 20, 2004.
19. Ibid.
20. 2004 election coverage, KIRO 710 Newsradio, Bonneville International Corporation, November 20, 2004.
21. Robert McGuire, email, November 20, 2004.
22. *Washington State Republican Party et al. v. Sam Reed*, U.S. District Court, November 20, 2004.
23. Nick Handy, email, November 22, 2004.
24. Ralph Thomas, "All Eyes on the State Recount," *Seattle Times*, November 23, 2004.
25. Nick Handy, email, November 23, 2004.
26. Concerns were expressed throughout the process over the manner in which counties reported the recount results. Because King County was the largest county, and the recount there would take longest, inevitably it was the last county to report. Some felt this put undue pressure on a county that reported last, therefore in the following year Secretary Reed proposed legislation that would allow for a uniform reporting time for election results. The legislation subsequently passed, codified as RCW 29A.64.061.
27. Office of the Secretary of State, "2004 Recount Update," press conference, November 24, 2004.
28. Ibid.
29. Ibid.
30. Ibid.
31. Ibid.
32. Ibid.
33. Kenneth Vogel, "Where the Heck Did Those Extra Ballots Come From?" *News Tribune*, November 25, 2004.
34. Ibid.
35. Associated Press, Akron *Beacon Journal*, November 25, 2004.
36. Associated Press, *Augusta Chronicle*, November 25, 2004.
37. 2004 election coverage, KIRO 710 Newsradio, Bonneville International Corporation.
38. Ibid.
39. Office of the Secretary of State, press conference, November 30, 2004.
40. Office of the Secretary of State, media advisory, November 30, 2004.
41. Office of the Secretary of State, "Reed Certifies 2004 General Election," press conference, November 30, 2004.
42. Ibid.
43. Governor Gary Locke, press conference, November 30, 2004.
44. Ibid.
45. Ibid.
46. The actual cost was $902,793.29, absorbed by the counties.
47. Press conference, November 30, 2004.
48. Ibid.
49. "Let Democrats Pay," *Post-Intelligencer*, December 1, 2004.
50. Ibid.
51. Ibid.
52. "Recount Yes, but Statewide," *Seattle Times*, November 30, 2004.
53. Ibid.
54. Peter Callaghan, "When Vote Count Favors other Party, It's Labeled Fraud," *News Tribune*, November 30, 2004.
55. Chris McGann, "Reed to Certify Rossi as Winner of Governor's Race," *Post-Intelligencer*, November 30, 2004.

Chapter Five

The Never-ending Campaigns

By December, two choices loomed. The Democrats could either finance a wholesale recount by hand, spending $730,000, or cherry pick by choosing ballots cast in Gregoire strongholds. State law only allowed for the party to receive its money back if the outcome changed, with Gregoire defeating Rossi. If the Republican candidate remained on top, the Democrats would lose $730,000.

As columnist Peter Callaghan pointed out, the consequences were steep—especially for Gregoire.

"If she pushes this battle to the end and still loses, what chance does she have to run again? And if she wins a third count and takes office, what damage does it do to her ability to govern effectively?"[1]

Later that day, Gregoire ended the speculation.

"From the beginning, this has been about getting all the votes counted so we can know for sure who won the Governor's race. So, my request of the state Democratic Party is simple: count the entire state or don't count at all. Counting every vote is the right thing to do."[2]

Some newspapers, such as *Seattle Times,* lined up behind her.

"The crystal-clear implication is she will concede if the party does not find enough money to do a statewide hand recount. That is appropriate and laudable."[3]

Others were not as generous.

"The *Tri-City Herald* editorial board recommended Gregoire to Mid-Columbia voters, in large part because of the work she has done to keep Hanford [nuclear] cleanup on track. Now we're asking her to concede the race and let the state get on with business."[4]

Elections never come cheap for supporters. But recounts, especially statewide hand recounts, puts an extraordinary cost on the shoulders of supporters, who are tapped dry come election time.

At 25¢ a ballot, with more than 2.8 million ballots cast, the Democrats scrambled to find the $730,000 payment. Defeated Presidential candidate John Kerry contributed to the cause.

"Kerry Backs Recount Effort in Governor's Race" noted the *Post-Intelligencer.*[5]

"John Kerry really came to our rescue," said Democratic State Chairman Paul Berendt. The former Presidential candidate contributed at least $200,000. "But our ability to pay for a statewide recount is still subject to money which is not in...We are

Seattle Post-Intelligencer

working to move heaven and earth to get all of the money we need."[6]

While fundraising efforts continued, the Democrats also worked incessantly to add confirmed votes to the pool of ballots that would be considered in the hand recount. Their first strategy was announced in correspondence to the Office of the Secretary of State. On behalf of the Democratic Party, Attorney David Burman sent a letter to Secretary Reed urging him to order counties to review all ballots, even those previously declared invalid and tossed out.

Burman argued that nothing in the law limited ballots in a recount to those that the local reviewing authorities (the county canvassing boards) deemed valid.

Burman claimed that statewide, election workers were using different standards to check voter signatures, and that King County was rejecting too many ballots overall.

"Disenfranchising people for sloppy handwriting is inexcusable, particularly when many of the rejections in King County were done by staff below the canvassing board level.

"Some other counties required that the board make every decision to reject a lawful vote due to insufficient matching of signatures."[7]

Finally, Burman claimed that Reed had more authority over the recount than he was willing to admit.

"As you know, we disagree strongly with such a limited view of your office's role, and we wonder why you are issuing guidelines at all if you are not going to help resolve these issues in a uniform statewide manner without requiring litigation."[8]

Predictably, the Burman letter did not sit well with either the Rossi campaign or the Republican Party.

Mary Lane, the Republican campaign's communications director, asserted that Burman's letter "raises the specter of Christine Gregoire, frustrated at not being able to win the election fair and square, trying to grab the governor's office by lawsuits and illegitimate ballot-counting." Lane also argued: "If Gregoire follows through on what her lawyers indicate in this letter, she would be blowing up the entire election process in this state… Gregoire's possible plan of suing her way into the governor's office should concern every Washington voter."[9]

From Secretary Reed's perspective, the laws were not the problem, and this recount would transpire like all others.

December 3

On December 3, the Democrats removed any doubt that the Gregoire-Rossi battle was continuing when sending a $730,000 check to the State. The official payment came with a formal request from Attorney David T. McDonald for a statewide hand recount.

"On behalf of the Washington State Democratic Party and related entities and all voters everywhere who cherish democracy, fairness, and open government," the submission letter read, "I hereby request that the State of Washington carry out a manual recount of all ballots submitted to State or County election officials by any elector of this state at any time in connection with the 2004 election of the next Governor of the State of Washington."[10]

Reed's office made the announcement: "Secretary of State Sam Reed Monday will issue a statewide manual recount order in the historic Governor's race between Governor-elect Dino Rossi and Attorney General Christine Gregoire."[11]

Again the election controversy earned national media coverage.

> **"Governor's Race Gets Second Recount"** proclaimed St. Paul's *Pioneer Press.*[12]

The Secretary of State's Office sent unofficial word of the hand recount to the counties, along with guidelines on how to proceed. Meanwhile, the elections community and the political parties and the candidates prepared to deal with the upcoming politically charged environment.

More complications came late that afternoon when the Democratic Party sued Secretary Reed in the State Supreme Court. In *McDonald* [Democratic Party] *v. Sam Reed* [Republican Party, et al.],[13] the Democrats called for rejected ballots to be put into the mix.

In their pleadings, Democrats sought "correction of unconstitutional

Preparing for a Hand Recount

Guidelines from the Office of the Secretary of State

- Canvassing Results—Counties must report manual recount results in the same manner as machine recount results.
- Preparation for the Recount—the two-day notice requirement is reiterated; sealed ballot boxes should not be opened prior to the two-day notice being satisfied.
- Recount Procedures—Counties could recount the ballots in any order.[1]
- Ballots—the County Canvassing Board has authority to recanvass certain ballots to correct discrepancies or inconsistencies in the returns. However, any recanvass must be completed prior to the last day to certify the count.[2]
- Security—Counties should provide security for off-site counting and use full security measures before and during the recount.
- Observers—There are statutory provisions regarding observers and their rights and limitations. [These were cited and augmented with recommendations including the importance of transparency and access as staff and space reasonably permitted.][3]

---

1. Democratic attorneys indicated they wanted to specify the order in which ballots would be recounted, yet no law existed for the Secretary to specify or require a specific order.
2. This particular statutory provision (RCW 29A.60.210) was key in all subsequent litigation resulting from the election. In November 2004, the statute read as follows: "Whenever the canvassing board finds that there is an apparent discrepancy or an inconsistency in the returns of a primary or election, the board may recanvass the ballots of voting devices in any precincts of the county. The canvassing board shall conduct any necessary recanvass activity on or before the last day to certify the primary or election and correct any error and document the correction of any error it finds." The statute has subsequently been amended to further clarify the authority of a canvassing board in these cases.
3. Office of the Secretary of State Staff, "Preparing for a Hand Recount," email to County Auditors and Interested Parties, December 3, 2004.

and other unlawful acts by election officials in the 2004 gubernatorial election and creation of rules by which county canvassing boards would conduct a hand recount of all votes cast in a manner that comports with Washington election law."[14] They argued that prior errors and inconsistencies by county canvassing boards should be reviewed, and the only way to accomplish that review was by a recanvass of every ballot cast in the election.

In media reports, Reed candidly addressed the case. A KIRO Radio news commentator asked:

"Secretary of State Sam Reed... We want to ask you first up about the Democrats going to the State Supreme Court to include these ballots that were rejected. How do you feel about that?"

The Secretary replied: "We've checked with our attorneys and a recount is exactly what it implies, which is you count once again the same ballots you counted before. So we don't expect them to prevail."[15]

As recount preparations continued, King County's Dean Logan asked the parties to appoint a participant to serve on each recount board, with a third person—a recorder—to be supplied by the county. He added that these workers would be considered county employees and paid. Also, Logan stated that five official political party observers would be permitted, also paid for by King County. Logan further specified: "We do not intend to limit the number of additional party and campaign observers...but we will restrict observers to certain areas during the recount."[16]

The Democrats felt this was inappropriate. "Party members will have conflicting obligations once they become county staff and will not be able to perform the role of witness/observer," they argued in their brief. "Even if the parties are able to assist the counties in staffing in this fashion, their rights to have witness/observers must be protected."[17]

Yet another concern expressed by the Democrats was that, in their words, no "uniform standards" had been

The Democrats' Arguments

In summary, the Democrats wanted a wholesale reinspection, or recanvass, of all ballots during the hand recount—including those already inspected and rejected by county canvassing boards.

In addition, the Democrats were unhappy with the "rules" for observers adopted by the Secretary of State.[1] According to the party, the rules would "prevent meaningful participation by party 'witnesses' in the hand recount."[2]

In particular, the party was concerned about the approach taken by Dean Logan, Manager of Records, Elections, and Licensing in King County. Logan had sent a letter to the Democratic and Republican county chairs on December 2, pointing out that the county planned on having 80 recount boards and that "for space and security reasons it is not possible to have observers from each party at every recount board table."[3]

1. In fact, the Secretary of State did not adopt "rules" in his guidelines for county auditors. Rather, he cited existing statutory provisions and made some recommendations to county auditors regarding observers. These recommendations essentially were that counties should accommodate observers whenever possible.
2. "Petitioners' Motion and Brief in Support of Emergency Partial Relief," p. 5.
3. Dean Logan, letter to Greg Rodriguez and Pat Herbold, December 2, 2004.

issued by the Secretary of State "for County Auditors to use in determining whether signatures are sufficiently different to justify rejection of a vote."[18] They felt signatures would be verified differently across the state. And, they had argued that some counties—King in particular—wound up with a higher invalidation rate because of this lack of a standard.

The Democrats were represented in this litigation by the Perkins Coie law firm. David Burman and Kevin Hamilton were appointed primary litigators.

Reed Disagrees with the Democratic Party

According to the Secretary of State, Democrats were asking for something State law did not authorize. First, the Democrats wanted every ballot re-examined—even those rejected in earlier counts. Second, they wanted political party observers to see every ballot. The party asked Reed to require that this be done in every Washington county.

But Reed argued that the Democrats failed to establish the point that the Secretary of State had such authority. He claimed they were attempting to issue new rules regarding the General Election of November 2.

Reed also clarified the definition of a recount. A recount, under State law, was not an opportunity to reexamine every ballot. No statute existed to support this interpretation. In a recount, only valid ballots could be considered.

Furthermore, standards already existed to address many of the Democrat's complaints, including the standards for what constituted an acceptable signature. "Petitioner's real complaint," the Secretary's brief stated, "is that they disagree with the decisions of some county canvassing boards under those statewide standards."[19]

Finally, Reed's brief clarified the "safety valve" in the law that allowed only certain errors to be corrected.

"To the extent that petitioners timely brought forward evidence of an unlawful inconsistency or error… RCW 29A.60.210…provides a safety valve for each county's canvassing board to correct such a timely raised and identified error. That limited safety valve for a particularly identified error, however, is not a floodgate requiring the wholesale recanvass of all ballots to see if perhaps any errors with respect to ballots might possibly have occurred. There simply is no constitutional or statutory bases for petitioners' demand that the 'recount' prescribed by the Washington legislature now be expanded to include, for example, a wholesale re-examination of signature verification issues previously submitted to and ruled upon by the county canvassing boards."[20]

The Secretary did not agree with the Democrats' interpretation of the statutes governing observers.[21] He pointed out that while the law clearly allowed observers, it did not authorize them to make decisions. The petitioners had not provided any legal authority for the court "to now re-write Washington's elections statute to add such privileges beyond the right to observe a recount as prescribed by the legislature."[22]

Secretary Reed concluded the summary of his brief with a request that the court deny the petitioners' motion and that it allow the hand recount "to promptly proceed without litigation, uncertainty, or delays so the People of our State can have a closure to this statutory recount process."[23]

Foster Pepper and Shefelman represented Secretary of State Sam Reed. Special Assistant Attorneys General Thomas Ahearne, Jeffery A. Richard, Hugh D. Spitzer, and Marco J. Magnano were assigned the case, with Ahearne serving as primary litigator.

The Republicans Intervene

The Washington State Republican Party and Governor-Elect Dino Rossi intervened in the Democrats' lawsuit.

While Republicans agreed with most of Secretary Reed's positions, they disagreed on the role of the county canvassing boards. They argued that the boards could only revisit discrepancies in the "returns"; they could not revisit errors made during the original count. The party believed the "returns" were *only* the numbers of reported ballots and votes. "Apparent discrepancies or inconsistencies in the returns from this election—the number of ballots cast and votes counted for specific candidates—do not provide a basis for the relief asked for by the petitioners," they argued.[24]

The Republicans were represented by the Davis Wright Tremaine law firm. Harry J.F. Korrell and Robert J. Maguire served as principal attorneys. Mark Braden, an attorney from Washington, D.C., also represented the interveners in this lawsuit.

The Key Differences

In court, key differences divided the major political parties and the Office of the Secretary of State. According to the Democrats, all ballots were subject to recanvassing by the canvassing boards for any reason.

Secretary Reed argued that some ballots could be added, but only those where discrepancies or inconsistencies were discovered in a timely manner or prior to the certification of the returns by the county canvassing board.

Republicans argued that only mathematical errors in the actual numbers—the "returns"—were subject to recanvassing.

"The state is fundamentally wrong in limiting the scope of the recount to merely the ballots that have already been counted," the Democrat's David Burman told the *Seattle Times* the next day. "We do think some mistakes were made in the original process...we want to make sure that [the recount] includes the areas that are most prone to mistake, and those are the subjective decisions that humans make."[25]

According to Reed, counties could reconsider ballots that had been rejected if there was a discrepancy. But the Secretary was not willing to accept the Democrats' position. "To suggest that we ought to reopen the entire process is quite inappropriate," said Reed.[26]

Attorney Mark Braden, representing the Republican Party and Dino Rossi, restated the position taken by the party in the litigation. "It's very simple, there is a recount process and that means you recount the ballots that were cast and put in the box. You re-open the box and you count the ballots again."[27]

Outside the court room, accusations flew.

The Rossi campaign alleged the Democratic Party was attempting to steal the election. "As far as we're concerned, it's trying to overturn the legitimate result of this election by any means necessary, ethical or not," Rossi spokeswoman Mary Lane said. "Christine Gregoire thinks more about her own political ambition than what the voters actually think."[28]

Republican Party Chairman Vance called the lawsuit "a nuclear bomb. It will blow up our election system in Washington State."[29]

December 6

On Monday, December 6, Secretary Reed officially ordered a hand recount of ballots cast for the State's highest office. An increasingly exhausting media schedule followed, with interviews often beginning as early as 6 a.m. and ending as late as 10 p.m.

Reed informed the counties that they could begin preliminary work, but asked that "in deference to the Supreme Court case, the counties not begin the recounting of the ballots until Thursday, or such date as the Supreme Court may provide."[30]

The twists and turns of the election left many shaking their heads. "What's happening in Washington could have occurred almost anywhere in the country," said Doug Chapin, director of electionline.org, a clearinghouse on election-reform news and information. "There are 49 other states…mopping their brows and saying 'Phew, it could have been us.'"[31]

Kirk Wolter, a University of Chicago statistics professor, stated: "There's a margin of error in connection with any measuring system, whether we're counting fish in a lake or counting votes for a governor." Professor Wolter had researched the Florida 2000 Presidential Election. In any election, he said, "there are millions of human interactions, and we're all human and we all make random mistakes."[32]

Jeffery Mondak, a political science professor at Florida State University, put it even more succinctly. "It's closer than the technology and our capacity as humans to decipher," he said. "You folks would do as well to flip a coin as to try and determine who actually won."[33]

Under the Media Glare The Hand Recount Begins

The counties, armed with a court order to push forward under existing recount rules, prepared for the daunting count of over 2.8 million ballots.

"Orderly Recount Pledged" noted Everett's *Herald* on December 7.[34]

"Why the Recount? And Is It Really Worth It?" questioned Bremerton's *Kitsap Sun*.[35]

To manage the enormous undertaking, King County settled into a new facility alongside Boeing Field and hired some 300 temporary workers. Workers would sort 334,000 poll ballots by precinct and nearly 564,000 absentee ballots into 17 legislative districts and then into 2,616 precincts.

Across the state, most counties would separate their ballots into six stacks, including votes cast for the three candidates, the overvoted and undervoted ballots, and the write-ins. The number of ballots in each stack would then be counted. As Reed noted in a recent press conference, election workers would endure intense pressure as the political parties and the campaigns watched and analyzed every move. He repeated: "Having been on the front lines, I can tell you about all of the pressure that's on you, the hours you're working, and the fatigue that sets in."[36]

Tiny Garfield County in southeast Washington, population 2,311, finished its recount first. On December 8, Garfield County reported no change in vote totals. Meanwhile, a number of the larger counties were still preparing to begin the recount.

As the week wore on, a few counties completed their recounts, adding votes for both candidates. In most cases, votes were added because election workers were able to determine voter intent in cases where the machines could not.

Some votes, however, were added for other reasons. Whatcom County discovered 7 additional provisional ballots, which had not been opened or counted in either the General Election or the first recount.

December 9

By the evening of December 9, ten counties had completed the manual recount, with a net change of 1 vote in favor of Rossi. Gregoire added 28 votes and Rossi 29.

Both campaigns pronounced themselves pleased.

"We've always said that with a by-the-rules recount, Dino will still be governor-elect,"[37] said Mary Lane, who also clarified the fact she was unconcerned about the almost 900,000 ballots remaining to be counted in the Gregoire stronghold of King County. "Gregoire has already wrung about as many votes out of King County as she can," Lane said. "King County, for all intents and purposes, has already done a partial hand recount."[38]

The Democrats also claimed satisfaction. The additional votes turning up in some counties had proven their point. "We've been saying from day one that every vote should be counted. With the race too close to call, this final count of the votes will allow the winner to take office with confidence," said Chairman Berendt.[39]

The Seattle Times

Long after any campaign effort could influence voters, public messages continued. Driving up congested Interstate 5, for example, motorists passed a large electronic billboard in Fife flashing the words: "Christine concede."

"From a corporate perspective, this would fall into the category of what we call reputation management," said Kurt Jacobson, president of JayRay, a Tacoma based public-relations company. "I think what the parties are doing is trying very hard to look good no matter what the result is."[40]

Jacobson believed that goal was harder for Democrats to achieve. After all, the party had run an aggressive campaign to find votes for their candidate, taking their case to court seeking judicial intervention.

"Democrats could have a hard time maintaining their image and winning," Jacobson said. "They can either be a graceful loser or a bruising winner."[41]

The public relations campaigns went on and on. The Democrats held a "Count Every Vote Candlelight Vigil," with the Republicans responding with a "Don't Change the Rules Rally." No December in the state's political history matched the twists and turns of this election.

Both parties successfully raised money. The Democrats raised more than $1 million, with the Kerry campaign and the Democratic National Committee each contributing $250,000. The Republicans raised almost $500,000 since the election—$300,000 coming after December 1.

King County Discovery

On December 13, the election already noted as one of the most sensational in recent Washington history took another dramatic turn.

> **"561 Valid King County Ballots Still Uncounted"** announced the *Post-Intelligencer.*[42]

King County election workers had discovered hundreds of mail ballots wrongly rejected. Numbering 561 altogether, they were eligible votes, but not included in any previous count. The voters' signatures on these ballots could not be verified in the county computer system because the names had inadvertently not been entered (an election staff oversight). Also, election staff had failed to next proceed to check the ballot signatures in the registered voters' original paper records on file. To his surprise, King County Councilman Larry Phillips stumbled upon his own name on the list of voters whose ballots were wrongly rejected.

"I was under the absolute impression [that] not only I voted, but followed the instructions correctly," said Phillips, a Democrat. "If it can happen to the King County Council Chairman, it can happen to anyone else."[43]

King County Elections Director Dean Logan prepared to ask the county canvassing board to count these "found" ballots and amend the certification.

"The mistake was on our part in not finding signatures of what appear to be eligible voters. We take full responsibility. An error has been made that has prevented valid ballots from being counted. We need to correct the error and count those votes."[44]

Arguments and Questions

Meanwhile, the day had arrived for the parties to make their case in court. The Democrats occupied one table at the State Supreme Court, while the Office of the Secretary of State and the Republicans shared a second table as respondents and interveners.

Democratic Attorney David Burman argued that King County's errors proved the need for all previously rejected ballots to be re-examined. Chief Justice Gerry Alexander countered with the argument that all valid ballots also be reconsidered. Alexander noted: "How can we say this is a systemic problem…without some fact-finding?"[45]

Thomas Ahearne of the Secretary of State's Office informed the court that the legislature knew what it was doing when it enacted laws for a recount—it was not to be a recanvass.

"The place to change the recount statute is in the Legislature, not this court," he said. "And the time to change the recount statute is before the election, not in the middle of the ongoing recount. Refusing to rewrite our State's recount statute is not an equal-protection violation."[46]

Mark Braden, representing the Republicans and Dino Rossi, put it directly. "Your election law is not a blank coloring book to be filled in at the desire of a candidate because they don't like the way a recount is going."[47]

It became evident the justices were anxious about inserting their power in the middle of a recount. The judges, mindful of the increased election litigation since *Bush v. Gore*, did not seem eager to travel that road. One exchange between the Democrat's Burman and Justice Bobbe Bridge seemed to reflect this. The justice asked Burman about the difference between recount and recanvass, and pointed out potential problems if either side should continually ask for the reconsideration

The Seattle Times

of rejected ballots. "How are we ever going to get finality in an election if that is the case?" she asked.

Burman responded that Democrats were in favor of finality, but it must be done fairly and correctly.

"Are voters supposed to take a lawyer now when they go to vote just to make sure everything is done correctly?" she continued.

"If they care enough, if they are worried enough about the errors, perhaps they should," Burman responded.[48]

December 14 The Decision

On Tuesday morning, December 14, the court rendered its decision in *McDonald et al. v. Reed et al.* The court unanimously rejected each of the major assertions made by the Democrats.

First, it stated that the process was clearly a recount, not a recanvass.

"Recount means the process of retabulating ballots and producing amended election returns. The procedure for recounts starts with the county canvassing board opening the sealed containers containing the ballots to be recounted. Thus, under Washington's statutory scheme, ballots are to be 'retabulated' only if they have been previously counted or tallied, subject to the procedures of RCW 29A.60.210.

"It follows that this court cannot order the Secretary of State to establish standards for the recanvassing of ballots previously rejected in this election."[49]

The court agreed with Secretary Reed that a safety valve did exist: errors made by election officials and discovered prior to certification could be corrected.

The court also ruled on the issue of signature checking standards.

"Petitioners call for uniform signature checking standards is beyond the relief that can be afforded in this action. Petitioners suggest that a claimed disparity in signature-checking standards implicates equal-protection concerns under the privileges and immunities clause of our state constitution, but they claim no discriminatory intent. We are mindful that King County rejected a higher percentage of signatures than did other counties, but the record before us does not establish the reason for this disparity, and it could be for factors other than the standard employed. We do not take petitioners' argument to suggest that a claimed disparity in rejection rates of voter signatures triggers some independent right, constitutional or otherwise, to a recanvassing of rejected ballots under a newly developed standard, nor does such an argument come to mind."[50]

Finally, the court addressed the rights of observers in recounts, and again supported Reed's position.

"As for petitioners' request that we order the Secretary to promulgate 'standards that allow party representatives to meaningfully witness the hand recount,' we are not convinced that such standards are presently lacking. RCW 29A.64.041 provides that the recount may be observed by persons representing the candidates, that these witnesses may make no record of the names, addresses, or information on the ballots, poll books, or applications for absentee ballots unless authorized by the superior court, and that the Secretary or county auditor may limit the number of observers to not less than two on each side if, in his or her opinion, a greater number would cause undue delay or disruption of the recount process. Petitioners provide no support for their suggestion that witnesses or observers are participants who have a right to be heard and influence this manual recount process."[51]

Thus concluded the first legal challenge to the mechanics of the recount process.

"I am heartened by the Court's decision," said Reed. "Stopping the recount to recanvass ballots would have set a bad precedent for the state of Washington. The voting process in our state is strong, but not perfect. During the next Legislative session, I will call for a series of reform measures to improve the way we vote and maintain voter confidence in the system."[52]

But voter confidence had suffered. Many people, such as KOMO Television commentator Ken Schram, held both party chairmen responsible.

"The political paranoia fostered by these two proves that they don't give a damn about the deep level of public cynicism they're helping to create.

"What they have done, and how they have done it, means that whomever ends up sitting in the governor's office will have one hell of an uphill job to do: Restoring public confidence that they even belong there.

"Way to go guys."[53]

And just as it seemed the elections process would now carry on smoothly, another 22 ballots turned up in King County.

Endnotes

1. Peter Callaghan, "Gregoire Must Consider Costs of Staying in Race," *News Tribune,* December 2, 2004.
2. Christine Gregoire for Governor Campaign, media statement, December 2, 2004.
3. "A Full Count, or None," *Seattle Times*, December 3, 2004.
4. "A Time to End Haggling over Governor's Race," *Tri-City Herald*, December 3, 2004.
5. Chris McGann, *Post-Intelligencer*, December 2, 2004.
6. Ibid.
7. Democratic Attorney David Burman, letter to Secretary of State Sam Reed, December 1, 2004.
8. Ibid.
9. Dino Rossi for Governor Campaign, "Gregoire Trying to Win Election by Lawsuit?" press release, December 2, 2004.
10. Democratic Attorney David T. McDonald, letter to Secretary of State Sam Reed, December 3, 2004.
11. Office of the Secretary of State, "Reed to Issue Recount Order Monday," media statement, December 3, 2004.
12. St. Paul *Pioneer Press*, December 4, 2004.
13. King, Pierce, Franklin, and Pend Oreille counties also were defendants, named as representatives for all of the county auditors and canvassing boards.
14. "Petitioners' Motion and Brief in Support of Emergency Partial Relief," p. 1.
15. 2004 election coverage, KIRO 710 Newsradio, Bonneville International Corporation.
16. Dean Logan letter, December 2, 2004.
17. "Petitioners Motion and Brief in Support of Emergency Partial Relief," p. 6.
18. Ibid., p. 3.
19. Ibid.
20. Ibid.
21. The Office of the Secretary of State held discussions with King County Elections Department regarding its proposed method of conducting the recount, making it clear in those discussions that, in their opinion, wherever possible observers should be given every opportunity to be meaningful witnesses to the proceedings.
22. "Washington Secretary of State's Response to Petitioners' Motion for Emergency Partial Relief," p. 4, December 7, 2004.
23. Ibid., p. 5.
24. "Interveners Opposition to Petition by Electors and Petition for Writ of Mandamus and other Relief and Motion in Support of Emergency Partial Relief," p. 26, December 7, 2004.
25. David Postman, "Suit Launches Battle over Ballots," *Seattle Times*, December 4, 2004.
26. Ibid.
27. Ibid.
28. Andrew Garber and David Postman, "Statewide Recount Next Week; Dems Sue over Rejected Ballots," *Seattle Times*, December 4, 2004.
29. Ibid.
30. Sheryl Moss, email, December 4, 2004.
31. Andrew Garber, "Top Vote-getter? We May Never Truly Know," *Seattle Times*, December 5, 2004.
32. Ibid.
33. Ibid.
34. Jerry Cornfield, Snohomish County *Daily Herald*, December 7, 2004.
35. Tim Botkin, *Kitsap Sun*, December 7, 2004.
36. Office of the Secretary of State, "Reed Certifies 2004 Governor Election," press conference, November 30, 2004.
37. Chris McGann, "Recount, Day 2: Rossi Still Leads," *Post-Intelligencer*, December 10, 2004.

38. Ibid.
39. Ibid.
40. David Postman and Andrew Garber, "Recount Rouses Donors, Spinners," *Seattle Times*, December 12, 2004.
41. Ibid.
42. Chris McGann, *Post-Intelligencer*, December 14, 2004.
43. Jennifer Sullivan and Keith Ervin, "King County Election Officials Will Take a Second Look at 561 Votes," *Seattle Times*, December 13, 2004.
44. King County Elections Department, "King County Identifies Previously Uncounted Ballots," press release, December 13, 2004.
45. David Postman, "Democrats' Lawsuit Unanimously Rejected by the State Supreme Court," *Seattle Times*, December 14, 2004.
46. Ibid.
47. Ibid.
48. Ibid.
49. *McDonald et al. v. Reed et al.*, 153 Wash 2nd 201, 103 P 3 722, December 14, 2004.
50. Ibid.
51. Ibid.
52. Office of the Secretary of State, "Reed Issues Statement on Supreme Court Decision," media statement, December 14, 2004.
53. Ken Schram, "These Dudes Need a Chill Pill," KOMO Television, Fisher Communications, Inc., December 15, 2004.

The only reasonable conclusion is to count as many votes as possible. Any other approach smacks of manipulating the election and disenfranchising voters.

Chapter Six

Hi Ho, Hi Ho... It's Back to Court We Go

With the clock ticking closer toward Christmas, the candidates, campaigns, and elections community traded precious shopping and family time for media interviews and damage control. As is typically the case with sensational, continuing news stories, reporters exhausted every means possible to turn out their reports. Media interviews continued to fill Secretary Reed's schedule. Repeatedly, reporters pushed for comment about the drama unfolding in King County.

On December 15, state and national reporters, two Federal Election Assistance Commission members, Secretary Reed, and several dignitaries squeezed into a standing-room-only county canvassing board meeting at the King County Administration Building in downtown Seattle.

The board would decide whether to include the 561 "found" ballots in the hand recount or reject them. The ballots, in Democratic leaning King County, might give Gregoire an edge and ultimately decide the excruciatingly close contest.

Every few minutes, the hearing room door opened with reporters leaving to attend to their scheduled live shots. New observers would crowd into their abandoned seats. Media outlets also broadcasted the hearing live.

At center stage were Dean Logan, Dwight Pelz, and Dan Satterberg of the county canvassing board. Logan, King County Elections Director, and Pelz, a King County councilman, were Democrats. The third member, Satterberg, Chief of Staff to Prosecuting Attorney Norm Maleng, was a Republican.

Their vote on the 561 ballots split along party lines—both Democrats opted to include the ballots, while Satterberg did not.

"I am heartened we have an opportunity to right a wrong," said Logan. "Clearly an administrative error was made in how these ballots were previously handled and presented to the canvassing board, and we have the clear authority under state law to review these ballots."[1]

Satterberg argued for a delay. "The factual basis that has been presented to us today [to justify verification of signatures] is...insufficient...The appearance to the world that's watching is that you're rushing this through."[2]

Republican Vance called the board's action "a 2–1 party-line vote in defiance of the King County Prosecutor's Office."[3]

Democrat Berendt said that the Republicans had not objected to counting overlooked ballots in counties that favored Rossi. "But now that the count isn't going their way, the GOP and Dino Rossi are screaming fraud in King County. They are doing everything they can to keep these ballots from being counted."[4]

The King County Canvassing Board planned to meet in a few days to determine the fate of another 22 ballots recently discovered in polling place units.

The debate over the 561 ballots did not end here. The Republicans tried to block the board's decision by seeking a temporary restraining order (TRO) from Pierce County Superior Court. The TRO would require King County to segregate the 561 absentee ballots, retain the ballots with each ballot envelope, and most importantly, prohibit King County from canvassing those ballots until a trial could be held on the merits of the case. In short, the TRO would stop King County from including the 561 ballots in its hand recount.

"This is a recount, not a recanvassing," argued Republican lawyer Diane Tebelius. According to Tebelius, State law only authorized recanvassing when there were overvotes and undervotes—the court should not allow hundreds of ballots to be added to the mix six weeks after the election.[5]

The Democrats disagreed. "If these votes had been counted originally, Christine Gregoire would probably be our governor right now," said a party spokeswoman. "We have to correct errors; that's the whole point of the recount."[6]

Republicans complained about poor security—alleging the 561 ballots were not secured properly and had been loosely carted from a satellite office to the King County Administration Building.

The crux of their case, however, hinged on the authority of the King County Canvassing Board. They asserted that the Washington State Supreme Court, in its decision the day before, held that no recanvassing could occur during the hand recount—or any recount. In effect, they felt this already rejected the 561 ballots.

King County fired back in arguing that the county canvassing board did have authority to correct errors and discrepancies in certain circumstances. "The King County Canvassing Board found that the returns for both the original count and the machine recount for the office of governor had an apparent discrepancy or inconsistency and…did not reflect the true number of valid absentee ballots that had been submitted for the November 2, 2004 General election.

"Just as was argued by the Washington Secretary of State's Office and as held by the Washington State Supreme Court this past Tuesday," the county continued, "the King County Canvassing Board had the authority, granted to it by the Legislature, to

Seattle Post-Intelligencer

re-examine or recanvass the ballots involved in the apparent discrepancy or inconsistency."[7]

In addition, King County rejected the claims about poor ballot security, calling them unsupported false accusations designed to confuse the issue before the court.[8]

The Democrats intervened and made the same arguments as King County.

Election mechanics and details in the voting process, which the public previously never knew or cared much about, suddenly were at the heart of the fierce political battle.

All the while, the average person's faith in the election process declined. The mounting number of errors, and the hostile tone of the criticisms leveled at King County, increased the tension.

In particular, critics directed their anger toward Dean Logan and Elections Superintendent Bill Huennekens. Yet many failed to mention Ron Sims, the King County Executive, who was elected by and accountable to the public for the successes and failures of the local election process. Sims played a major role in budget decisions and logistics that had impacted elections in Washington's largest county for years.

Said Chairman Vance of the latest development in King County, "it's either gross incompetence or vote fraud…there's no way to tell if they are colossally incompetent or totally corrupt."[9]

"I do think that this situation has shaken voter confidence in King County," said Dean Logan. "And that's disheartening to me because…we've just worked extremely hard to rebuild that level of trust. I just feel awful about that situation."[10] Interestingly, Logan had found himself attacked and defended by both parties at different times during the election. He was initially sued by the Democrats, and verbally chastised in the media by them, for not releasing the names of provisional voters during the original count. He was praised and defended by the Republicans for taking that position. Later, the Republicans had cited, with approval, his position that a hand recount was not as accurate as the completed machine recount.[11]

Now, the situation was reversed. The Republicans made allegations of incompetence and possible fraud, while Democrats took a more conciliatory tone. "We're human beings. We make mistakes and what's important is that the mistakes be corrected," said Gregoire spokesman Morton Brilliant.[12]

The same was true of Secretary Reed, who alternately found himself praised or vilified by one political party or the other, depending on his position and how either candidate fared at the time.

Reed earlier defended King County, but now, following these latest revelations, he expressed "deep" concern following the discovery of additional ballots. "I think unfortunately it reflects the fact that this is a county that has had some real problems with its election operations for years," he said. "The problems in King County aren't problems of lack of good policy or lack of guidelines. It's a problem of execution."[13]

Reed's comments were taken personally by many election workers, including Logan, who Reed had once personally hired as State Elections Director. The Secretary felt that despite his tremendous respect for Logan, he could not honestly defend the county. In his opinion, the situation went beyond normal mistakes to unacceptable practices.

December 17

Voter mistrust toward King County escalated when election workers turned up more mishandled ballots.

"Another 162 ballots have been misplaced in King County," announced Jane Shannon of KIRO News Radio.[14]

As a King County sheriff's deputy stood guard, election workers had unlocked a cage inside a Seattle warehouse and thoroughly searched the plastic trays. They uncovered a batch of mail ballots marked "no signature on file."

KIRO News Radio's Chris Sullivan updated listeners. "These are absentee ballots just like the 573 found on Monday."[15]

At the time, King County Elections staff estimated there were "150" absentee ballots in total, not counted in either the original count or the machine recount and cast by voters whose last names generally began with A or B.

(The discovery would bring the total number of mishandled ballots in King County to 723, further eroding public trust.)

King County Elections Superintendent Bill Huennekens said the 150 ballots, like the 561 found earlier, were mistakenly rejected because of a problem scanning the voters' signatures into the county's computer system.

"It is a serious mistake that we've made but we're going to do the right things for the citizens of King County," said Huennekens.[16]

"I'm not sure there's a word in the English language strong enough for this. Fiasco, circus, joke," remarked Republican Party Chairman Chris Vance.[17]

But the very same day, to the surprise of most, a court decision in Pierce County gave Republicans new hope. Pierce County Superior Court Judge Stephanie Arend granted the Republican Party's request to halt King County from adding the hundreds of recently discovered ballots.

Judge Arend based her decision on whether the absentee ballots could be included in the recount. She concluded, in light of the State Supreme Court decision, no recanvassing could take place.

Arend decided that the 561 ballots already had been canvassed and rejected, and now could not be considered by the King County Canvassing Board. Arend did not rule on the accusations of poor ballot security.

Specifically, Republicans were granted a temporary restraining order to stop election workers from taking the newly discovered ballots out of their outer envelopes bearing the voter's signature.

The court battle continued. Logan announced plans for an appeal, and Supreme Court Chief Justice Gerry Alexander said the high court was prepared to take up the case the following week.

"Every day is up for grabs, except, I guess, Christmas Eve, which is a state holiday this year," Alexander said. "We're conscious of the need to move with all deliberate speed on this."[18]

Rossi spokeswoman Mary Lane said Arend made the right decision.

"If King County were allowed to keep adding more ballots, elections would never end," Lane said.[19]

But Gregoire declared in a statement: "From the beginning, this has been about fixing mistakes and counting every legitimate ballot. The people of Washington deserve an accurate count."[20]

Even more upset over the superior court decision was King County Councilman Larry Phillips, who had discovered by happenstance the ballot signature errors in the first place when his own mail ballot was among the rejected. When processing Phillips' mail ballot, the elections staff had not found his signature in the computer system scan, and failed to go to his voter registration card on file to check for it, as required by standard procedures.

"Through no fault of my own, I have just been disenfranchised," Phillips said. "It's a travesty."[21]

Revote

During this period, the notion of holding a new election was born. Support for a revote grew in such popularity that a campaign began with activists championing and defending the new cause with bumper stickers and signs.

"How about a do-over," noted KOMO Television.

Ralph Munro, Washington's former Secretary of State for 20 years and a key Rossi supporter, was the first to suggest holding a second election.

"This thing could just degenerate and spiral downward," Munro said. "Whoever eventually becomes governor is going to have a very hard time governing, and we're going to go through four years of flopping around."[22] Munro suggested allowing a period of time for new voter registrations, and then holding a new election in February.

The idea garnered great appeal among the Rossi faithful, as well as the average voter tired of the harsh rhetoric or "mistake du jour" that seemed to surface in this election.

The obstacle to a revote was the fact that "do-over'" elections were nowhere authorized in State law or the constitution. Some citizens, continuing the tradition of misperceptions about the power and authority of the Secretary of State's Office, thought Reed could simply order a new election, resolving the situation. Many became upset when Reed pointed out he simply did not have that authority.

Nor was it clear if anyone else did. Reed said a second election was mechanically do-able, but he theorized that either the legislature or the courts would have to order it. He personally thought a second election was preferable to having the entire recount drag on through the judicial process, and then having the Governor ultimately selected by the courts. Reed maintained that the Washington Governor ought to be chosen by the people, not the courts.

"I'm still hoping that when we get done with this recount, we'll have a clear winner and can get on with the transition," he said. "I think we'd be better off if that happened."[23]

Chairman Vance seemed open to the possibility of a new election. "Perhaps the only way we're going to settle this is to let the people of Washington vote again," he said.[24] The Democrats were far less interested in a new election. "Last week the Republicans were saying we need to resolve this as quickly as possible," Democratic Party spokeswoman Kristin Brost said. "This week they're saying we need another election."[25]

Meanwhile, the hand recount continued. On December 17, with just King, Pierce and Spokane counties left to report, Gregoire trailed Rossi by just

74 votes. The political parties punched up their rhetoric. Democrat Berendt labeled Rossi the "accidental governor-elect." He argued that the only reason Rossi led after the first recount was due to King County's errors, and, now that the errors were being corrected, the Republicans wanted to stop the process.[26] He also took the Republicans to task for flip-flopping their position on the court role in elections.

"Last week, Rossi's mantra was, 'I trust people, not lawyers,'" Berendt said. "Now that all the votes are being counted and he's afraid of falling behind, he's rushing into court, putting his personal ambition before the rights of the voters."[27]

Round Two

Washington State Republican Party et al. v. King County et al.

King County immediately petitioned the State Supreme Court for review of the Pierce County Superior Court decision blocking the processing of the newly discovered absentee ballots. The Washington State Democratic Party and Secretary Reed joined in the appeal as intervener-petitioners.

Reed wanted a clear interpretation from the court regarding the authority of county canvassing boards to correct mistakes before certification. He believed this authority existed. He had taken the same position in the first State Supreme Court case, and now did so again when intervening in this next case before the court.

Meanwhile, many Republicans accused Reed of betraying his own party and siding with the Democrats. The *Seattle Times*, however, reported that "Reed maintains that King County has the same right as every other county to correct errors during the recount."[28]

The argument advanced by the three petitioners (King County, the Democrats, and Reed) was simple—Pierce County Superior Court had incorrectly interpreted the original December 14 decision by the State Supreme Court in the original case, and that far from prohibiting the King County Canvassing Board from recanvassing the absentee ballots, it specifically permitted such a recanvass.

The brief submitted by King County underlined a key part of the State Supreme Court's decision in citing RCW 29A.60.210, and concluded: "The Superior court ignored the underlined portion of this sentence and instead concluded that this Court ordered that no recanvassing can occur in the manual recount regardless of RCW 29A.60.210. The Superior Court's interpretation of this Court's Opinion Order is incorrect and removes the clear discretionary authority the Washington Legislature granted to county canvassing boards to recanvass ballots pursuant to RCW 29A.60.210."[29]

Tom Ahearne, counsel for Secretary Reed, submitted a motion asking for the court to clarify the wording of its December 14 opinion order, so as to "make it clear that in connection with the ongoing recount process, canvassing boards do have the discretion under RCW 29A.60.210 to correct previous errors where the canvassing board finds an apparent discrepancy or inconsistency in the returns that a recanvassing of specific ballots can correct."[30]

In fact, in his brief, Ahearne cited dialogue between himself and the court during the earlier case when the 561 ballots were discussed and where the issue of RCW 29A.60.210 serving as a safety valve was explained. Counsel also pointed out that if, in fact, that statute did not exist as a safety valve, then a number of certified county returns from the machine recount would not be correct, since many counties had relied on that statute to correct errors and discrepancies during the count.

Editorials—Partisan, Irrelevant Things

It was becoming apparent to everyone that the disputed King County ballots would be critical to the outcome of the second recount. Most believed, if these ballots were included, Gregoire's chances of prevailing were significantly increased. Should they be excluded, then the opposite would hold true. Both Seattle newspapers weighed in on the question in editorials. Although endorsing different candidates prior to the election, both unequivocally recommended counting the disputed ballots.

"In a recent ruling largely against the Democrats," the *Seattle Times* opined, "the State Supreme Court said ballots are to be retabulated only if they have been previously counted or tallied, subject to a specific provision of Washington law. That provision says county canvassing boards ought to fix errors if the board finds an apparent discrepancy or inconsistency in the returns.

"This safety valve exists to correct exactly the kind of mistakes discovered in King County.

"This page endorsed Republican Dino Rossi for governor. Adding the King County votes to the mix may push his opponent, Democrat Christine Gregoire, over the top.

"But the only reasonable conclusion is to count as many votes as possible. Any other approach smacks of manipulating the election and disenfranchising voters who did what they were supposed to do and cast their ballots in good faith."[31]

The *Post-Intelligencer* took the same position the following day. In its editorial, the paper encouraged the court to keep an eye on the ultimate goal.[32]

"For Republican Party Chairman Chris Vance, the goal is to elect Dino Rossi," it concluded.

"For Paul Berendt, his Democratic Party counterpart, the goal is to elect Christine Gregoire.

"Ignore those goals. As sincere as those men may be in the pursuit of their goals, these are partisan, irrelevant things. The goal is to accurately as possible determine the will of the governed, as represented by the ballots cast by the voters. Even in pursuit of that goal, some ballots must be excluded; ballots of those voters who failed to sign them or get them in on time, voted twice or were blatantly incorrect in marking their ballots or failed to make their intent clear.

> *"The goal is to accurately as possible determine the will of the governed, as represented by the ballots cast by the voters."*

"The ballots of those voters who cast them correctly and on time but were not tallied because of elections officials' errors must be counted now… There is no sustainable argument for disenfranchising these voters."[33]

On Wednesday morning, December 22, the State Supreme Court heard oral arguments in the appeal of the Pierce County Superior Court decision, which had halted the canvassing of the disputed 723 absentee ballots. Harry Korrell, representing the Republicans, argued that counting those votes would cause irreparable harm, but several of the justices questioned exactly who would be hurt.

"You're looking at it from the point of view of the winner or the loser—shouldn't we be looking at it from the point of view of the voter?" asked Justice Susan Owens.[34] Each party in the case made arguments consistent with their well-known position on the critical question before the court—the extent of authority of the county canvassing boards. Oral arguments concluded at around 11 a.m.

The court ruled quickly and unanimously, confirming that the recanvassing statute authorized a canvassing board to recanvass specific ballots upon a finding of an inconsistency or discrepancy in the returns, whether those ballots had been counted previously or not.

The court made particular note of the fact that "the canvassing board has concluded that the returns as made may indeed be 'actually incorrect.' The board also says that further examination of the ballots under question may well show details 'different from those contained upon the returns.'"[35]

The court went on to say that the Republicans wanted a narrow interpretation of the words "an apparent discrepancy or an inconsistency in the returns" so that it meant only an arithmetic error disclosed on the face of the returns themselves, but that this was contrary to the Court's previous holding in an earlier case (*State ex. rel. Doyle v. Superior Court of King County,* 138 Wash. 488, 244 P 702).

"Moreover," the court continued, "since the statute permits recanvassing, it is instructive to remember that canvassing involves 'examining ballots or groups of ballots, subtotals, and cumulative totals in order to determine the official returns' RCW 29A.04.013. Here, certain ballots were coded as having 'no signature on file' without having been fully examined to properly place them in that category. In that sense they were never fully canvassed, and the seeming error in placing them in any category has become evident to the King County Canvassing Board. Under *Doyle* this is just the sort of apparent discrepancy or inconsistency that the board can correct through recanvassing."

In conclusion, the court ruled: "It thus follows that the superior court erred in granting a temporary restraining order, and that the King County Canvassing Board properly concluded that it had authority to recanvass the subject ballots pursuant to RCW.29A.60.210."[36]

The 723 absentee ballots were, by virtue of the court's ruling, now going back into the ballot pool. Assuming the ballots were valid, they would be added to the count. King County reported the results of its completed hand recount on the afternoon of the court's decision. Minus the 723 ballots yet to be opened, the statewide cumulative totals now showed Chris Gregoire leading by 10 votes. King County had yet to certify its final numbers by adding the valid votes from the 723 absentee ballots still left to canvass.

Republicans, clearly unhappy with the court's ruling, vowed to seek out Rossi votes in the other counties where election workers also had rejected valid votes, but Secretary Reed warned they

Justice Chambers

Included with the majority decision, written by Justice Alexander, there was a spirited concurrence by Justice Chambers.[1] He concurred fully with the judgment and reasoning of the court, but wanted to express his opinion on a broader subject. He expressed concern about the courts intervening in elections "before matters are placed on the ballot, before people vote, and before election officials have fulfilled their duties to canvass and count the votes."

Chambers felt "there is little to commend judicial intervention into the electoral process before the process is complete. First, the necessary procedures of judicial decision making do not lend themselves to instant resolution of electoral issues."

He concluded, courts "should be reluctant…to issue temporary restraining orders or grant emergency review of election matters before election officials have had sufficient opportunity to fulfill their duties… The legislature should make the law, the courts should interpret the law, and the executive should execute the law. The legislature has empowered county election officers and canvassing boards to administer elections. For courts to micromanage election officers is to inappropriately blur the executive and judicial functions of government."

1. *Washington State Republican Party et al. v. King County et al.*, 153 Wash 2d 220, 103, P 3d 725, December 22, 2004.

were too late. "The counties don't have the authority now to do that," he said. "The statute says specifically that you have to do this by the day of certification in the county. They have now certified and they're through."[37]

Republican Chairman Vance said that the ruling fundamentally changed the rules for elections, but again Secretary Reed disagreed, stating that the ruling upheld election procedures that had been in place for decades.[38]

The following day, King County certified its returns, including the valid votes from the disputed absentee ballots (566 of the ballots ultimately were included in the count, with Gregoire adding 311 votes and Rossi 191). Vote adjustments also had been made in a majority of the other counties.

The final returns showed Christine Gregoire prevailing in the State Governor's race by 129 votes.

The first press reports listed the margin as 130 votes, but the difference was explained by what occurred in Thurston County. Thurston County followed up its initial certification of the manual recount with an amended certification, which added the ballot of one voter—as it turned out, 1 vote for Christine Gregoire. However, the Office of the Secretary of State refused to accept the amended certification on the grounds that there was no statutory authority for any amending of the returns once the canvassing board signed the certification form.

Press reports began to surface that the Republican Party, following the State Supreme Court's decision, intended, in the words of the media, to "mine for more votes" by contacting counties and asking them to reopen their certified election returns. The party hoped the canvassing boards in those counties would find inconsistencies or discrepancies in the returns and add more ballots to the pool. In some instances, what had occurred in Thurston County was cited as an example.

Early in the evening of Wednesday, December 22, State Elections Director Nick Handy sent an email to all of the county auditors stating the position of the Office of the Secretary of State.

"We want to advise you that the position of this office is that the ability of a canvassing board to 'recanvass' exists up to the point that the county 'certifies' its results. (See RCW 29A.60.210). 38 counties have certified results to this office.

"Thus, in our view, the door is legally closed on your ability to recanvass at this point. King County, of course, may still recanvass as it has not yet certified. King County is expected to certify Thursday at 3 p.m."[39] The email also suggested that any prosecuting attorney who wished to do so could contact Secretary Reed's attorney, Tom Ahearne, to discuss the matter.

On the following day, a letter was sent by the Republican Party to at least some county canvassing boards, citing the State Supreme Court decision and asking that the board "recanvass ballots that were mistakenly excluded from your tabulation and returns during the initial canvass and recount, pursuant to your authority under RCW 29A.60.210. Specifically, we request that you recanvass and tabulate ballots from the voters who confirm, by the attached declarations or in person, that they are properly registered voters who signed and timely cast ballots in this election."[40] It seemed as though the Republicans were misreading the decision by the State Supreme Court.

While a number of county canvassing boards declined to meet with the Republicans and consider their request, at least four did. But each of the four boards declined to re-open the canvassing process, citing State law. A fifth board cancelled its scheduled meeting and said it would not consider the Republican request. An email from Gary Zandell, the Lewis County Auditor (and like all other members of the Lewis County Canvassing Board, a Republican), summed up the position of that county's board.

"The Lewis County Canvassing Board met at 8:45 a.m. today to review the request from the Washington State Republican Party to reopen the canvass of the November election and consider including nine ballots/affidavits from voters whose ballots had been rejected because of signature illegibility.

"Following a public discussion of the Supreme Court decision, correspondence from the Lewis County Prosecuting Attorney's Office, Secretary of State, and various statutory provisions, the canvassing board reluctantly but unanimously rejected the request from the Republican Party."[41]

Ultimately, no county canvassing board complied with the Republican request to recanvass previously rejected ballots. The final statewide vote total stood as follows:

Gregoire	1,373,361
Rossi	1,373,232
Bennett	63,465

The ballots cast for the chief executive of Washington State had been counted and certified. There were no *administrative* remedies left for Dino Rossi and the Republican Party to pursue. The *legal* remedies, however, were far from exhausted, and emotions directed at Secretary Reed began to boil over.

Endnotes

1. King County Elections Department, "Logan Issues Statement on Canvassing Board Decision," press release, December 15, 2004.
2. Neil Modie, "King County Board Moves to Verify 573 Ballots," *Post-Intelligencer*, December 16, 2004.
3. Keith Ervin and Susan Gilmore, "New Look at 573 Ballots May Close Gregoire Gap," *Seattle Times*, December 16, 2004.
4. Ibid.
5. Rebecca Cook (for the Associated Press), "Court Considers Newly Discovered Ballots in Governor's Race," *Seattle Times*, December 17, 2004.
6. Ibid.
7. "Defendants Response to Motion for Temporary Restraining Order," p. 2, December 17, 2004.
8. Ibid.
9. David Postman, "Cascading Errors Shake Voter Confidence," *Seattle Times*, December 16, 2004.
10. Ibid.
11. Ibid.
12. Ibid.
13. Ibid.
14. Jane Shannon, 2004 election coverage, KIRO 710 Newsradio, Bonneville International Corporation, December 17, 2004. Initially, King County estimated it pulled 150 ballots from the cage. Media reported the figure as 162. The final number reported by King County Elections was 174.
15. Chris Sullivan, 2004 election coverage, KIRO 710 Newsradio, Bonneville International Corporation, December 17, 2004.
16. Associated Press, "Judge Blocks Count of Some Washington Ballots," *USA Today*, December 17, 2004.
17. Robert Mak and Mike Cate, "Trial and Error," KING TV special report, June 15, 2005.
18. "Democrats Appeal to Supreme Court to Count Rejected Ballots," KING Television, Belo Corporation, December 19, 2004.
19. Ibid.
20. Ibid.
21. Ibid.
22. Ralph Thomas, "Former Secretary of State Pushes for New Vote," *Seattle Times*, December 17, 2004.
23. Ibid.
24. Ibid.
25. Ibid.
26. Chris McGann, "Gregoire Trails by 74 with 3 Counties Left," *Post-Intelligencer*, December 17, 2004.
27. Ibid.
28. David Postman, "Reed Says County Has Right to Fix Error, Tally 735 ballots," *Seattle Times*, December 21, 2004.
29. "King County's Statement of Grounds for Discretionary Review," p. 6, December 21, 2004.
30. "Washington Secretary of State's Motion to Clarify This Court's December 14 Opinion Order," p. 1, December 21, 2004.
31. "Count the Votes in King County," *Seattle Times*, December 21, 2004.
32. "Keep Eye on the Goal," *Post-Intelligencer*, December 22, 2004.
33. Ibid.
34. Rebecca Cook for the Associated Press, "King County Reports Recount Results: Gregoire by 10," *Seattle Times*, December 22, 2004.
35. *Washington State Republican Party et al. v. King County et al.*, 153 Wash 2d 220, 103 P 3d 725. December 22, 2004.
36. Ibid.
37. Chris McGann, "Third Time May Be Charm for Gregoire," *Post-Intelligencer*, December 23, 2004.
38. Ibid.
39. Nick Handy, email, December 22, 2004.
40. Peter Schalestock, letter from Washington State Republican Party to Grays Harbor County Canvassing Board, December 23, 2004.
41. Gary Zandell, email, December 28, 2004.

Media outlets sized up the news reports of 2004 and called the feud over the chief executive's office the biggest political story of the year.

Chapter Seven

Making the Case

Anyone assuming the hand recount would conclude the 2004 election drama was sorely mistaken.

As the major political parties waged war in the media, voter confidence in Washington's elections sunk further. Each day, it seemed a new allegation emerged as the Republicans called into question every facet of the election, targeting in particular the Gregoire stronghold of King County.

Media outlets sized up the news reports of 2004 and called the feud over the chief executive's office the biggest political story of the year.

> **"A Look Back: Tight Governor Race Easily the Top Story"** noted Seattle's *Post-Intelligencer.*[1]

Although many questioned the legal validity of some of the charges now being presented, no one could dispute the effect on public opinion resulting from the accusations of conspiracy and the attacks on election procedures.

The Republicans leveled multiple allegations at King County. They argued that a flawed ballot enhancement process favored Gregoire, that many in the military were denied the right to vote, and that the county canvassing boards—which refused to take a second look at previously rejected ballots—were unfair. (It is worth noting that the party never formally appealed those canvassing board decisions.)

"The decisions today [of county canvassing boards to not recanvass ballots] highlights the fact that there is inconsistency across the state in the way disenfranchised voters are treated," said Rossi spokeswoman Mary Lane.[2]

At the same time, the Republicans began building their case. From King County, the party sought:

- A list of all voters who participated in the General Election and the fate of their ballots.
- All documents that related to the issuance, delivery, or counting of military and overseas ballots.
- Emails and other correspondence to or from all county workers connected in any way to the 2004 election.
- Complaints from voters who had problems receiving their ballots.
- Envelopes and other voting materials that related to rejected absentee and provisional ballots due to problems with voter signatures.

> **"GOP Wants Vote Data from King County"** reported the *Post-Intelligencer.*[3]
>
> **"GOP Demands Voter List"** noted the *Bellingham Herald.*[4]

The *Post-Intelligencer* urged the political parties to be patient.

A long series of press conferences kept the media and public updated throughout the election contest. *The Seattle Times*

"It's particularly important for the Republicans to conduct themselves in a methodical, disciplined fashion.

"Republicans may want to focus their pursuit of additional voting information on King County. They would serve the state better by asking how well the election was conducted statewide, including those areas that supported Dino Rossi."[5]

But at a press conference that very evening, Republican Dino Rossi urged Democrat Christine Gregoire to join him in a call for a second election.

"The uncertainty surrounding this election isn't just bad for you and me—it is bad for the entire state," Rossi announced when reading a letter he sent to Gregoire. "People need to know for sure that the next Governor actually won the election. A revote would be the best solution for the people of our state, and would give us a legitimate governorship."[6]

Rossi's bid for a second vote made the national news.

> **"New Election Is Sought in Washington"** noted the *Los Angeles Times.*
>
> **"In Washington, Call for a Second Election"** announced the *New York Times.*[7]

The Democrats, flush with victory after an agonizing two-month battle, held a much different view. Unlike the Republicans, of course, it was they who now had a Governorship to lose. A Democratic spokeswoman called Rossi's request "absurd." "In one breath he says that drawing out the process would hurt the state and in the next he says he wants a do-over. It would be spending $4 million because he doesn't like the results of this election."[8]

The next morning, approving articles appeared regarding Reed's impending certification of the hand recount.

"Reed has not acted as an agent of his political party or its candidate. His only loyalty has been to Washington voters.

"Throughout the past eight weeks, Reed has proven a model of fairness, good judgment, and honesty. In contrast to what happens in many states, the Republican has shown that a partisan official can administer even the closest election in an even-handed manner."[9]

Accolades, however, did not come from the inner circles of the Republican Party. The bitterness among party insiders grew that day as Reed accepted the election results, giving Gregoire the Governor's office by a mere 129 votes. Had he not done so, however, he would have violated his oath of office.

Concluding the elections process marked the end of two exhausting months spent on three separate counts of more than 2.8 million ballots.

"I think some thanks and acknowledgements are due," Reed told the media as cameras flashed in his Olympia office. "First to the voters of the state of Washington for their patience and their understanding as we are working our way through the clos-

Election Returns, the Secretary's Duty, and the Law

"The returns of every election for the officers named in the first section of this article shall be sealed up and transmitted to the seat of government by the returning officers, directed to the secretary of state, who shall deliver the same to the speaker of the house of representatives at the first meeting of the house thereafter, who shall open, publish and declare the result thereof in the presence of a majority of the members of both houses. The person having the highest number of votes shall be declared duly elected, and a certificate thereof shall be given to such person, signed by the presiding officers of both houses; but if any two or more shall be highest and equal in votes for the same office, one of them shall be chosen by the joint vote of both houses. Contested elections for such officers shall be decided by the legislature in such manner as shall be determined by law. The terms of all officers named in section one of this article shall commence on the second Monday in January after their election until otherwise provided by law."

(RCW 29a.60.190, Certification of election results—Unofficial returns; RCW 29a.60.230, Abstract by election officer—Transmittal to secretary of state; and RCW 29a.60.250, secretary of state—Final returns.)

est statewide election in the history of the state of Washington."[10]

Reed also thanked the candidates. "I myself have been a candidate a number of times and I've been through a recount and such. You cannot imagine what it is like on your stomach, what it's like trying to go to sleep at night after you have given so much of your life for an entire year or more to a race and see it come down to this."[11]

The election was—as Reed pointed out—more than 99 percent accurate. But the imperfections left plenty of room for a court challenge and Reed supported Rossi in such a decision.

"Senator Rossi has a right to pursue a challenge of this election through the election contest statutes," said Reed.

If given the choice, Reed also clarified that he would choose a revote over a court selection of the Governor. "The people have a right to decide who their next chief executive is for the state of Washington, if we end up with an election set aside."[12]

Finally, Reed announced that he would soon introduce legislation to clear up the State's elections process. Most important among the detailed proposals was simply changing the timing of the State Primary to an earlier date. Though Reed had pushed for an earlier Primary date for years, the recent election, if nothing else, proved what difficulties could ensue if this was not done. A late Primary date simply did not allow election workers

The Seattle Times

enough time to fully prepare for early November's General Election.

> "**New Governor Is Certified**" ran the *Cincinnati Post.*[13]

The crowning of Washington's 22nd Governor, picked up by media nationwide, proved to be the nail in the coffin in the opinion of many Rossi supporters. Clearly, an expectation existed for Reed to stop the elections process because of the number of errors that had occurred—especially in populous and liberal King County. Even some of the Secretary's closest advisors were convinced that Reed owned much of the blame for Rossi's loss.

On January 3, animosity toward Reed spread across the Sunday edition of the *Seattle Times*. Someone had turned a personal email sent to Reed over to David Postman, the *Times*' chief political reporter. Written by one of Reed's closest advisors, the email had been sent to the Secretary's entire "kitchen cabinet," which advises on his performance as Secretary of State.

"How convenient to blame 'emotions' for the mass discontent within Republican ranks over your handling of the major legal issues in this gubernatorial recount," John Giese wrote to Reed and his fellow members of the kitchen cabinet.

"I am one of those who has no intentions of supporting you in the future either, because you didn't listen."[14]

Reed, who came from a long line of Republicans, was still optimistic that feelings of ill will would fade with time.

More Ballots than Voters?

Meanwhile, a story surfaced that added to the growing list of Republican charges against King County. In response to a public disclosure request, the county released a list of its registered voters broken down by those who were credited with participating in the election and those who were not. A conservative blogger discovered a discrepancy between the number of voters credited with voting on the county's list and the number of ballots actually counted. The county reported 899,199 ballots cast, which turned out to be 3,539 more than the number of people credited with voting.[15]

Elections Director Dean Logan explained that this was not unusual—counties generally resolve these discrepancies right after the election. But in 2004, this was impossible due to the two recounts, public disclosure requests, and the harsh glare of the media spotlight.

"I think that historically the data has never been reconciled 100 percent between ballots cast and the voters given credit for voting," Logan said. "I think 3,500 is higher than what I'm comfortable with...I would be less concerned if we were in the range of 1,000 or 1,200."[16]

Across the state, election officials agreed, explaining that the record of credited voters—at least with respect to poll site voters—was a post-election process conducted to update voter registration files.

"I'm approaching my 29th year in elections and cannot remember ever achieving a one-for-one reconciliation [one ballot counted = one voter credited]," began Lewis County Auditor Gary Zandell in an email to the *Seattle Times'* David Postman. "The crediting process is done on the fly as daily mail ballots are returned and after the poll books are returned from the polling place. The crediting is done by whatever staff member or temporary hire is available. The crediting of a voter is a mechanical process, accomplished by passing a wand over a unique voter registration number on the return label of a mail voter or that same number in a poll book. Some clerks use a key pad to enter this six digit number... In the meantime, the phone is ringing, customers are needing help at the counter, or nature calls. In a nutshell, a number is easily transposed or omitted in error."[17]

The crediting of voters was a dynamic process. After election results were certified, counties reopened the voter registration lists. They deleted voters and added new voters to update and clean the registration lists. A list of registered voters from November 15 would not match a list of credited voters dated December 15. And neither would likely match the number of ballots cast on November 2.

* * *

Stories now also began to appear regarding the legislature and its heretofore pro forma ratification of the election returns, which was scheduled to occur on January 11. Republican House Minority Leader Bruce Chandler said that unless questions were answered about the election process, Republicans planned to object.

"It's not about the result," Chandler said. "The rules were not followed and that's something the legislature should take very seriously."[18]

On the other side of the aisle, Senate Democratic leader Lisa Brown said election officials followed the rules and that the Republicans were upset because their candidate lost.[19]

But Wait...There's More... the Unverified Provisional

More allegations of wrongdoing emerged in what Republican Chairman Vance labeled a bombshell. Vance alleged that on election day, election workers counted hundreds of provisional ballots without first verifying if the ballots were cast by eligible voters. "I think the only way of settling this certified mess of an election is a revote."[20]

A Republican-appointed election worker appeared at a press conference, saying he personally witnessed about 150 to 300 provisional ballots go straight into tabulating machines on election day without any voter verification.

"Given this new revelation... Christine Gregoire should join with Dino Rossi in asking the Legislature to call a new election," Vance continued.[21]

"The effort right now is a public-relations campaign," replied Democratic Party spokeswoman Lisa Cohen. "They're throwing something against the wall and seeing what may stick."[22]

Elections Director Dean Logan responded to the GOP accusations, calling the provisional ballot problem exaggerated. "It's absolutely true that we know there were places where provisional ballots were put through AccuVotes. There is nothing that indicates it was fraudulent or an intent to create havoc with the election system."[23]

"It's not fraud. It's not understanding how the elections process really works and then it's this stirring of the pot with inaccurate information," said Carolyn Diepenbrock, Snohomish County elections manager.[24] She added that the 300 vote discrepancy in her county was probably due mostly to human errors in the tedious, labor-intensive, post-election process of entering general election voters' names into the files.

"I would like to say that there should never, ever, ever be any discrepancy. But that's not reality. It's unfortunate that this [voter] crediting process is being attached to the election process, because they are separate, unrelated procedures."[25]

It seemed many Republicans were convinced there was a conspiracy afoot to rob them of the Governorship. This was especially true of talk-radio hosts and conservative bloggers, who followed every hiccup of the election drama. The level of criticism, already harsh and intense prior to the certification of the hand recount, now was ratcheted up several notches. In a lengthy column, editorial columnist Joni Balter in the *Seattle Times* took conservative talk radio to task for its "we were had" approach to the unfolding story.

"On many of these shows," she wrote, "hyperbole is king. Words are loaded. Conspiracy theories are highly encouraged. Hours go by with a constant pitch for a new vote between Rossi and Gregoire...Obviously some people involved in talk radio are well informed and well read, including several hosts who clearly do their homework...Yet talk radio, by its spontaneous nature, often is unburdened by facts.

"The Republican attack on the election is by now a near-military operation—air, land, and sea. Scour death records to find dead voters. Search records to find felons who voted in violation of the law. Compare the number of voters to votes cast. Hold the outraged—OUTRAGED!—press conference du jour. Do anything to put Rossi back on top. No matter what.

"With Republicans in control of the White House, U.S. House, and Senate, it is challenging for some talk-show hosts to find enough compelling material to get riled up about. Their gang is in power and they have to find something more than unsightly national deficits and an ill-advised war.

"Serve up the closest governor's race in state history, one with decisive votes coming out of the most liberal and richest county, and you have something very close to talk-show heaven."[26]

The Dead

Allegations of deceased voters casting ballots emerged in King County. The *Post-Intelligencer* initially found 8 mail ballots cast by deceased voters in the county. In at least one case, an elderly woman admitted she voted for her husband, who died October 7, nearly a month before the General Election. Because he was blind, she had power of attorney for him and admitted to signing her husband's name and mailing his ballot along with her own. Another man admitted to voting for his deceased wife, who died September 29. Still another deceased man was credited with voting and his wife was not, even though she stated that she did vote. King County verified she had simply voted on her husband's ballot, since she had not returned one herself, and King County accepted the ballot as hers. Other instances were under investigation by the county at the time the *Post-Intelligencer* story ran.

The Washington State Health Department admitted it only sent out lists of deceased citizens "every two to three months." The last effective listing was sent to county auditors on May 5, 2004, six months before election day.[27]

"If we don't receive a notice that they're dead, then we have no way of taking them off the" county election

Theater over the election brought spirited protests to Olympia, including this demonstrator mocking the "dead" who voted.
Ellen M. Banner/The Seattle Times

rolls, said Dean Logan. He added that "relatives of the deceased can and do cancel some registrations."[28]

Though the number of deceased voters casting ballots was small, the findings added another sensational aspect to the 2004 election dispute. In most cases, these instances turned out to be elderly persons casting a ballot for a deceased spouse, or, in some instances, election officials simply credited the wrong person. However, the cumulative affect of such stories continued to chip away at public confidence in the election process.[29] And more was to come.

Felons

The elections flap continued next with accusations over illegal felon voting. Tom McCabe, Executive Vice President of the Building Industry Association of Washington (BIAW) and a long time Gregoire political foe, had assembled voter registration and convicted felon data to determine how many illegal ballots possibly were cast.

According to an article in the *Seattle Times*, McCabe compiled an initial list of 48 suspects in Pierce County by matching names and addresses. A subsequent review by the *Seattle Times* found 19 possible felon voters and confirmed that 2 actually had voted. The other 29 did not match in other ways, such as by birth date. Of 64 Snohomish cases identified by McCabe, the *Times* analysis found that 13 did not match.

McCabe experienced a great deal of difficulty and obstacles in compiling his numbers. For example, no list existed of those felons with restored civil (including voting) rights that could be readily compared to registered voter lists. Lists indeed existed of people charged with felonies, but, in some cases, plea bargaining had reduced their charge to a misdemeanor. Other lists showed those currently incarcerated. But none identified those felons whose civil (and voting) rights had been legally restored.

As illustrated in the *Kitsap Sun*, obtaining accurate information regarding felon voting is difficult at best. BIAW had provided an initial listing of 11 potential felon voters in Kitsap County, which the *Kitsap Sun* decided to investigate. Of the 11 names investigated, the following facts were revealed:

- Two had their voting rights restored.
- Four did not vote.
- One had voting rights stripped after the election.
- Two voted, but it could not be confirmed whether they had had their voting rights restored, or whether they had voted illegally.
- Two voted illegally.[30]

Military and Overseas Voters

There also was an attempt to blame election officials for failing to mail ballots soon enough for people in the military to vote. Rossi went so far as to hold a press conference with the

Felons and Voting

As allegations arose of felons voting in the election, the State became embroiled in a bitter dispute. This highly controversial issue also was one of the most complicated.

Under Washington law, felons lose the right to vote. However, once they have fulfilled all sentence obligations (such as fines, probation, rehabilitation, or other requirements cited by the court), they can restore their voting rights by completing a formal process under the law.

No government entity, however, tracks the two specific felon populations—those who restored their voting privileges, and those who have not. This is in large part due to the complexities and wide variety of criminal sentences.

Adding to the problem was the fact that many felons assumed that, once they served jail or prison time, their voting rights were automatically restored. Other felons did not realize they lost their right to vote in the first place.

Felons could restore voting rights by following different procedures, depending on where and when they were convicted.

- For felons convicted by a Washington State court for a crime committed after July 1, 1984, the Department of Corrections would notify the sentencing court and the court would issue a Certificate of Discharge, restoring voting rights.
- People convicted by a Washington State court for a crime committed before July 1, 1984, would petition the Indeterminate Sentencing Review Board to restore their voting rights.
- For felons convicted in federal court, the Washington State Clemency and Pardons Board had the authority to restore civil rights.

To complicate matters further, each state had its own laws regarding felon voting rights. In Maine and Vermont, for example, felons did not lose their voting privilege. In every other state, they did—for a period of time. Felons eligible to vote in the states where they were convicted would be eligible to vote in Washington, as long as they met all other State registration requirements.

Felons pardoned by the Governor or the President automatically have their voting rights restored.

Election offices depended on the courts to notify them if a person was convicted of a felony, and on voters to know whether their rights had been restored.

(Washington State Constitution, Article VI, Section 1).

parents of a Marine wounded in Iraq, who did not receive his ballot until the day after the election. The story was featured on radio ads calling for a new election.

Another soldier, however, offered a different consideration.

"I would be willing to bet...that 95 percent of the people in my platoon, company, and battalion did not receive a ballot," said Marine Corporal Ted Lester from Snohomish County. "The other five percent did, but they received them burned beyond recognition and about 4–5 weeks too late." He described the mail system in Iraq as a "joke," and claimed one mail truck was blown up a week before the election.[31]

King County reported that in addition to sending mail ballots to many military and overseas voters, they emailed and faxed ballots to others to make sure they received them on time. A number of other counties did the same. King County also reported issuing 15,289 military and overseas ballots, of which 12,694 were returned.[32]

The Battle Is Joined— *Borders et al. v. King County et al.*

On January 7, Dino Rossi took the momentous step of filing suit in Chelan County Superior Court, formally contesting the election of Christine Gregoire. The suit was initially assigned to Judge T.W. Small, one of three Chelan County judges, and asked the court to set the Governor's contest aside and order a new election. "The number of illegal votes counted, and the number of valid votes improperly rejected in this election are so great as to render the true result of the election uncertain and likely unknowable," the lawsuit claimed.[33] The lawsuit, however, did not ask the court to prevent the swearing in of Gregoire as Governor.

Gregoire reacted calmly. "I respect the rights of others to file an action in court. That's their right."[34]

She considered the problems arising in the election were simple mistakes and said no fraud was involved. Rossi seemed to agree, in somewhat of a departure from the Republican rhetoric then filling talk radio. Rossi argued, however, that according to State law, errors can be grounds for setting aside an election. He emphasized that he was not alleging a conspiracy gave the election to Gregoire, and that no one "is out to steal the election."[35]

In their suit, Republicans argued that thousands of illegal voters were counted statewide because of "errors, omissions, misconduct, neglect, and other wrongful acts" by election officials.[36]

The suit named as defendants the state's 39 counties (each county auditor individually), Secretary of State Sam Reed, Speaker of the House Frank Chopp, and Lieutenant Governor Brad Owen. It listed a number of plaintiffs who were "residents and electors," including Chris Vance, Chairman of the State Republican Party, and the

Public opinion regarding the Governor Election soared to new heights when protesters broadcasted their discontent over the outcome.
Office of the Secretary of State

Rossi for Governor Campaign ("a candidate committee"). Mr. Borders was included as one of the "residents and electors," in *Borders et al. v. King County et al.*

"If you can't tell who won an election because of errors and mistakes, you have to rerun it," said Harry Korrell, a lawyer for the GOP.

Democratic Chairman Berendt had a different take. In his opinion, the Republicans would have to prove—and as yet had not—that the problems would have changed the outcome of the election.[37]

The Legislature Meets

Washington's legislature convened on January 10, 2005. In addition to dealing with a projected revenue shortfall of at least $1.6 billion, the battle over the Governor's office was a top priority.

Most lawmakers agreed that the legislature's debate over the acceptance of the election returns would only be symbolic in nature. The Democrats controlled both houses and any attempt to delay or set the returns aside was likely to split down party lines.

"We're all kind of cringing, waiting until Tuesday gets over with," said Democratic State Senator Darlene Fairley. "The bottom line is a revote isn't going to happen. The House and the Senate are solid" Democratic.[38]

Senate Minority Leader Bill Finkbeiner wanted to delay the process. The Republican said "the Legislature needs to ask, 'Do we rush through, do we quickly certify and ratify this election, or do we wait and act deliberatively and get to the bottom of these issues?' This is going to be a four year term; we can wait two more weeks."[39]

Finkbeiner's proposal was rejected on a 25–24 vote, with only one Democrat, Tim Sheldon, voting with the Republicans. He too echoed the revote call.

"I've heard from my constituents overwhelmingly, that they think there are so many irregularities that the only way to resolve it is with a revote," Sheldon said.[40]

The following day, January 11, in a joint session the Washington State Legislature confirmed the election of Christine Gregoire as Washington's 22nd Governor. The Speaker of the

House, Democrat Frank Chopp, had opened the floor to debate. Republicans argued to wait two weeks before approving the election, but this effort failed by a margin of 80–65. Only one Democrat, Senator Sheldon, a maverick, voted with the Republicans.[41]

Just outside on the capitol steps, pro-Rossi protesters held a revote rally, holding signs mocking the gubernatorial election and some of its star players. Some protestors dressed as skeletons, representing the "dead" voters who cast ballots.

A much smaller group of Gregoire supporters held a counter rally, urging that the election results stand. The Washington State Patrol kept the peaceful but boisterous groups apart. The two demonstrations altogether totaled about 3,000 people.

At the rally, Chris Vance energized Rossi supporters by listing all of the allegations of errors and wrong doing that had appeared in the press since the certification of the original election. Bob Williams, head of the conservative Evergreen Freedom Foundation, apparently not in agreement with Rossi's statement that no one was out to "steal the election," called on the FBI to impound King County's election records and to turn the matter over to a federal grand jury.

The Reverend Ken Hutcherson of the Antioch Bible Church in Redmond sounded the most ominous tone. "You can give us a revote or you're going to cause a revolt," he warned.[42]

In arguing against any delay, Representative Jeannie Darneille, a Tacoma Democrat, said that past lawmakers had the wisdom to set up a process for settling close elections.

"We are in the midst of that process," she said. "It's been long, it's been laborious, it's been fractious but it's been constitutionally mandated.

"Now we are being faced with this motion to defer...our acceptance of the certification that was made by our secretary of state.

"Do we feel we have been deceived? Are our courts deceiving us? Was the election rigged? Our courts will decide."[43]

Endnotes

1. *Post-Intelligencer,* December 29, 2004.
2. Chris McGann, "Counties Deny GOP's Plea to Reconsider Rossi Votes," *Post-Intelligencer*, December 29, 2004.
3. Chris McGann, *Post-Intelligencer*, December 28, 2004.
4. Associated Press, *Bellingham Herald*, December 28, 2004.
5. "A Vote for Calm," *Post-Intelligencer*, December 29, 2004.
6. "New Election Is Sought in Washington," *Los Angeles Times*, December 30, 2004.
7. Sarah Kershaw, *New York Times*, December 30, 2004
8. Ibid.
9. "A Model Secretary of State," *Oregonian*, December 30, 2004.
10. Office of the Secretary of State, "Reed Certifies Gubernatorial Recount," press conference, December 30, 2004.

11. Ibid.
12. Ibid.
13. Associated Press, *Cincinnati Post,* December 31, 2004.
14. David Postman, "Republican Reed Faces GOP Wrath over Recount Decisions," *Seattle Times*, January 3, 2005.
15. David Postman, "Doubts Linger as Gregoire Win Certified," *Seattle Times*, December 31, 2004.
16. Ibid.
17. Gary Zandell to David Postman, email, January 5, 2005.
18. David Postman, "Doubts Linger as Gregoire Win Certified," *Seattle Times*, December 31, 2004.
19. Ibid.
20. Neil Modie, "GOP Announces 'Bombshell' in Voting," *Post-Intelligencer,* January 6, 2005.
21. Keith Ervin, "GOP Says Hundreds of Ballots Suspect," *Seattle Times*, January 6, 2005.
22. Ibid.
23. Ibid.
24. Neil Modie, "GOP Announces 'Bombshell' in Voting," *Post-Intelligencer,* January 5, 2005.
25. Ibid.
26. Joni Balter, "Lighting Up the Phone Lines with a We-were-had-lament," *Seattle Times*, January 6, 2005.
27. Another listing was sent November 1, 2004, obviously too close to the November 2 General Election to be used by the counties.
28. Phuong Cat Le and Michelle Nicolosi, "Dead Voted in Governor's Race," *Post-Intelligencer,* January 7, 2005.
29. The creation of a state database, brought online for the 2006 elections, should greatly reduce the opportunity for this to happen in future elections, and eventually may eliminate the possibility entirely.
30. Kitsapsun.com, January 27, 2005.
31. Ibid.
32. Ibid.
33. Chris McGann, "Rossi Files Suit for a New Vote," *Post-Intelligencer*, January 8, 2005.
34. David Postman, "GOP Suit Doesn't Ask to Prevent Swearing-in," *Seattle Times*, January 8, 2005.
35. Ibid.
36. Ibid.
37. Chris McGann, "Rossi Files Suit for a New Vote," *Post-Intelligencer,* January 8, 2005.
38. David Ammons (for the Associated Press), "'New Beginning' as Lawmakers Ring in New Session," *Seattle Times*, January 10, 2005.
39. Ibid.
40. Chris McGann, "GOP Bid to Stall Gregoire Is Turned Back," *Post-Intelligencer,* January 11, 2005.
41. Chris McGann and Kyle Arnold, "Divided Joint Session Certifies Gregoire Governor-elect," *Post-Intelligencer*, January 12, 2005.
42. Ralph Thomas and Andrew Garber, "Two Side Rally on Eve of Inaugural," *Seattle Times*, January 12, 2005.
43. Chris McGann and Kyle Arnold, "Divided Joint Session Certifies Gregoire Governor-elect," *Post-Intelligencer*, January 12, 2005.

In a press conference on January 6, 2005, Secretary Reed discusses methods to revamp our election system and solve some of the problems.
Office of the Secretary of State

As the court case began, there came a series of legal motions asking for, among other requests, a new election should the Republicans prevail—or a dismissal of the entire case should the Democrats win.

Chapter Eight

Charges Leveled as Court Fight Looms

Although Gregoire was inaugurated, Rossi and the Republicans moved forward with the election challenge in the courts.

In their petition to Chelan County Superior Court, Republicans purported that because so many gross oversights clouded the 2004 Governor's election, it was impossible to tell whether the people put Christine Gregoire in office or Dino Rossi.

"The court should declare the election void, set it aside, order that any certification of the results of the election and any certificate of election issued as a result of the election are also void, and order that a new election be conducted as soon as practicable."[1]

Mindful that not a single Democrat held office in Chelan County and that Rossi carried that area by 63 percent of the vote, Democratic Party Chairman Paul Berendt accused the Republicans of judge shopping.

"It was obvious that they decided to go to the most conservative county in the state that has the most conservative judges in the state," claimed Berendt.[2]

Not so, said Republicans, stating they chose Chelan County because it promised a quicker trial date and a fairer venue due to its considerable distance from troubled King County.

As the court case began, there came a series of legal motions asking for, among other requests, a new election should the Republicans prevail—or a dismissal of the entire case should the Democrats win. How the judge would consider these requests was anyone's guess.

"The results are so close, and so many questions have been raised, that it is impossible for me to predict the outcome of the contested election case with any confidence," admitted Reed, an elections expert with more than 35 years of experience, including the administering of numerous close recounts.[3]

The Republican Party argued that nullifying the Governor's election was the only plausible solution, and accused election workers of:

- Counting more ballots than people credited with voting.
- Counting unverified provisional ballots.
- Counting ballots cast by felons whose right to vote had not been restored.
- Counting votes submitted in the name of deceased people.
- Counting votes cast by people other than the voter whose name was signed on a ballot.
- Failure to ensure that military, overseas, and other voters received their ballots in a timely manner.

- Violating equal protection rights by refusing to correct mistakes in some counties while correcting errors in others.
- Violating equal protection rights by allowing third parties to solicit, collect, and present ballot signatures.
- Violating equal protection rights by failing to establish and follow uniform standards regarding enhancement and duplication of ballots.
- Violating equal protection rights by failing to provide consistent standards for the treatment of overvotes and undervotes.[4]

On January 10, the Democrats officially entered the court battle. The

The Venue and the Judges

On January 10, Judge T.W. Small of the Chelan County Superior Court, to whom the case was "randomly assigned," sent a letter to all attorneys involved in the litigation, disclosing his connections to some of those involved. Small offered all opportunity for being asked to recuse himself from hearing the case. He asked that any such request be made to his court reporter.

"To facilitate the parties' free exercise of this right to request recusal, she [the court reporter] has been directed not to disclose to this court what party requested recusal...Upon notice of such a request, the court will recuse, without need to file an affidavit of prejudice."[1]

When a scheduled hearing was held in Chelan County on January 12, Judge John E. Bridges appeared rather than Judge Small. Judge Small had recused himself after Franklin County submitted a request that he do so.

Thus, John Bridges, a 58-year-old Chelan County native, was assigned the historic case.

In 1988, Governor Booth Gardner appointed Bridges to the superior court. Most observers did not consider Bridges to be "political." However, Bridges had great appeal to Dale Foreman, a Republican, for presiding over this case. Foreman, a former state Republican chairman and State Representative, joined the Republican legal team for the election contest case.

Five years earlier, Foreman represented the Mayor of Wenatchee when the mayor's election was challenged. Bridges presided over the trial and overturned the election—something the Republicans were anxious to see repeated.

At the preliminary hearing in the high-profile case, Judge Bridges approved unopposed motions allowing both the Democrats and the Libertarians to intervene in the lawsuit, and then postponed a scheduled preliminary hearing for one week, presumably to allow himself time to become familiar with the case.

1. Judge T.W. Small, letter to counsel, January 10, 2005.

motion to intervene argued that they had "a substantial interest in ensuring that the results of this election stand."[5]

Democrats disputed the call for a new election. "Were the court to grant Petitioners' request, all Democratic and Republican legislators and state-wide office holders would also have to stand for re-election because of Article III, Section 1[6] of the State Constitution."[7] According to this section of the constitution, Washington's executive officers should be elected at the same time as members of the legislature.[8]

Not surprisingly, the Democrats took exception to most of the Republican claims. They justified their involvement by stating that Secretary Reed had refused to refund their $730,000 recount deposit until the election contest was resolved. Lastly, the party argued that despite shared views between the respondents in the case and the Democratic Party, the respondents could not adequately represent the Democrats' interests in court.

The Teams

With the swearing-in of new Attorney General Rob McKenna, the Attorney General's Office played a key role in the election contest case. McKenna became Secretary of State Sam Reed's attorney. He assigned veteran Assistant Attorney General Jeff Even to the case. Reed also retained Tom Ahearne, a Foster Pepper and Shefelman attorney who played a preeminent role in successfully representing the Secretary in two State Supreme Court cases.

Attorneys David Burman, Kevin Hamilton, Jenny Durkan, and Russ Speidel represented the Democrats.

The Republican team included Seattle attorneys Harry Korrell and Robert Maguire, Mark Braden from the Republican National Committee, and Attorney Dale Foreman of Wenatchee. Foreman was a prominent figure in Washington politics, having served as chair of the Republican State Committee and as Republican Majority Leader in the State House of Representatives. He unsuccessfully ran for Governor in 1996.

More Legal Maneuvers

Meanwhile, Republicans continued the daunting task of gathering evidence, which buried the counties and the Office of the Secretary of State under a mounting number of public disclosure requests.

On January 13, attorneys for Rossi and the Republican Party asked the Washington State Patrol for an electronic copy of its criminal database, which contained more than 1.2 million records regarding people charged with felonies and misdemeanors. Democratic Party Attorney Jenny Durkan took exception to the Republicans' request.

"I find it beyond offensive that exercising your right to vote would trigger any kind of criminal background check," said Durkan. "If the State did this, it'd be a huge violation of civil rights."[9]

Setting the Stage for the Historic Trial

In preparation for court, the parties filed numerous legal motions. Republicans tried for expedited discovery. They asked that local and state election officials be given 2 days' notice, instead of the usual 5, to give pretrial testimony, and that records and other data be produced within 10 days instead of the usual 30. The Democrats, most counties, and the Secretary of State opposed this motion.

Meanwhile, the Democrats attempted to put a stop to the discovery process. According to the party, the court needed to settle outstanding issues first. Democrats claimed that if the court resolved them against the Republicans, the intended discovery would be irrelevant. Reed took the middle ground, that discovery should continue but at a reasonable pace, and not on an accelerated schedule.

Additionally, four counties—Benton, Snohomish, Jefferson, and Lewis—filed a request that they be dismissed from the lawsuit, which had named all 39 counties. They argued that the Republicans had made no claims against these four counties, therefore they were not proper parties to the lawsuit.[10]

January 20 Hearing

On January 20, the consequential hearing began in an old auditorium across the street from the Chelan County Courthouse in Wenatchee. This unusual venue accommodated the large number of lawyers involved in the case, as well as the extensive media participation it was sure to attract.

A significant number of prosecutors appeared in person to present their arguments, and even more participated by conference call. The key parties in the case—the Republicans, Democrats, and Secretary of State—were each represented by their respective legal teams.

The Republicans began by arguing for an expedited schedule in scouring county election documents for mistakes. The more quickly this information could be obtained, said the party, the more quickly it could show enough errors to nullify the election of Gregoire and the need to hold another vote.

"We simply want to put the facts before the court; let the truth come out," said Republican Attorney Rob Maguire. "It's hard to dispute that there is a cloud over the legitimacy of these election results."[11]

Democratic Attorney Jenny Durkan countered that the Republicans were asking the court for permission to "rummage through the cemeteries and retirement homes looking for deceased people and people vacationing in Phoenix half the year," who voted in the election. "It's their burden to come forward with demonstrable proof that this election should be set aside."[12]

County Overload

Meanwhile, by conference call, Jefferson County's David Alvarez claimed that the public disclosure requests would shut down his elections department for two solid weeks.

"They are asking us for documents we do not have," added an attorney from Kittitas County. "They want to give us the burden of making their case. If they want to expedite [the discovery requests,] it should be focused. It should be relevant, and it should not change from day to day."[13]

The Republicans said they were open to compromise, and did meet 10 counties' needs by greatly reducing the amount of information that their elections people would be expected to produce. The party offered to narrow their subpoenas, drop lawyers' fees, and remove the counties' as parties in the suit—except the county auditors. For their part, the counties would be required to quickly turn over information and not oppose Rossi's call for a new election—should Judge Bridges invalidate the election.

This approach did not sit well with a number of prosecuting attorneys who refused to accept the deal. Island County's Greg Banks accused the Republicans of "extorting stipulations out of the counties," and claimed it was unfair to ask for more evidence from "counties that didn't knuckle under to this."[14]

The Decision

In his denial of the Republicans' request for expedited discovery, Judge John Bridges argued that accelerating the collection of evidence could lead to chaos and injustice.

"The old maxim that justice delayed is justice denied has a corollary," said Bridges. "And that is justice hurried is justice denied."[15]

Bridges also refused the counter request to suspend all discovery until major legal and jurisdictional questions could be answered. However, Bridges did concede that some of the Democrats' questions must be quickly resolved. He issued a tight deadline for the filing of briefs on those questions, and set February 4 as the day he would hear arguments on the Democrats' motion to dismiss the case altogether.

All the while, the Republicans were pressing on with their public demonstration to prove that hundreds of illegal votes were cast in the 2004 election. They contended that the number of illegal votes far exceeded Gregoire's narrow victory margin.

Meanwhile, the media began focusing on the complications in monitoring the voting rights of felons. The *Seattle Times* zeroed in on some of the problems: When a person is convicted of a felony, the court clerk notifies election officials in the same county where the conviction occurs. Administrators then remove the felon's name from the voter registration lists, but difficulty can arise when matching a felon's name in the voter registers. There is no use of a common identifier, such as a driver's license or Social Security number, if a felon shares the same or similar name with a registered voter. Also, a person may be convicted of a felony in one county, but be registered in another county.

The list of complications surrounding the felon voting issue is long. When voters sign their registration form, they affirm the statement that they had not lost their civil rights due to committing a felony. Voters sign the statement under penalty of perjury. Many felons, however, do not read the statement carefully, or do not realize they had lost their civil rights. Dean Logan of King County concluded, "I don't think it's the responsibility of election administrators to essentially do background checks on registered voters."[16]

Pat McCarthy, the Pierce County Auditor, said this would not even be possible. "We don't have the capacity to do that, and that's true of every county in the state."[17]

One of the difficulties faced by felons after being released from incarceration was that the voting prohibition continued until all sentence obligations were satisfied, including any financial requirements that might have been imposed by the court.[18] Many simply did not know they were still not eligible to register and vote.

This was illustrated by one felon still owing $132,000 in restitution, but who had cast an absentee ballot, not knowing that is was illegal for him to do so. He was particularly upset about this, as well as with the Governor's election dispute, and concluded: "Up until now I thought my vote counted and my wife's vote counted. Now I realize the system is crooked. I don't think we will vote any more."[19]

On Thursday, January 27, specific allegations were presented by the Republican Party, which claimed to have discovered 300 illegal votes and more than 400 others that could not be verified. A confident Chris Vance said he expected the number to "literally grow every day."[20]

Included among the alleged 300 illegal voters were 240 said to have been cast by felons—the bulk of whom were registered in King County. An additional 44 were identified as votes cast under the name of deceased people, 10 voters allegedly voted twice, and 6 voted in Washington and another state.[21]

Democrats claimed they were not concerned about the Republicans' revelations. Their attorneys argued that most of these problem voters, including felons, were improperly registered and should have been challenged before the election. "There's no proof that Dino Rossi won the election, and that's what you need to show," said Democratic Party spokeswoman Kristin Brost.[22]

Election Fight Will Go Forward

On February 4, Judge Bridges declared that the Republican Party would have its day in court.

"The case should go forward, at least at this point," pronounced Bridges from the Chelan County Superior Court.[23]

"We'll be able to present our evidence, and we'll be able to get to the bottom of the problems with this election," an encouraged Dino Rossi told reporters.[24]

The news was not good for Democrats, who had hoped Bridges would deny the case because Republicans had "utterly failed to establish the daunting grounds required."[25]

Specifically, the Democrats were relying on four main arguments to put an end to the election contest:

- The Republican Party must clearly prove the election was invalid.
- Voter registration challenges should be made before an election.
- The discrepancy between the number of people credited with voting and the number of ballots actually cast was irrelevant.
- Claims that provisional ballots were counted before determined eligibility were also irrelevant because: "Provisional ballots are required by law to be counted in the absence of clear and convincing evidence that the recipient was not qualified."[26]

Finally, Democrats argued that election errors happen in every contest, and "what is missing from the petition is equally notable. There is no allegation that there was any fraud or wrongdoing by election officials or that Governor Gregoire...participated in any fraud or wrongdoing.

"They argue that voters seeking to set aside elections...can merely accumulate a series of good faith errors by election officials to justify their claim. With all due respect, this is not Washington's law and it never has been."[27]

The Republicans fought back, relying mostly on an old court case defined in the Secretary of State's brief.

In his brief, Reed had defined an illegal vote as it relates to the election contest statute. Although the Democrats argued that voter registration challenges should be made before the election, Reed had reminded the court of RCW 29A.68.020 that allowed correction.

In its definition of an illegal vote, the statute specifically included "a vote cast by a person disqualified under article VI, section 3 of the state constitution," and when more than one vote was cast by a single voter.[28]

The Secretary also cited the constitutional provision that "bars from the franchise convicted felons [until their civil rights are restored] and those individuals judicially declared mentally incompetent...Since voters in those categories...are specifically included within the scope of the illegal voting concept, the language that follows should not be read to exclude them."[29]

The Reasoning of the Court

Judge Bridges was not convinced by the Democrats, calling their claim premature that the Republicans had failed to prove the election invalid.

With respect to whether election contests must proceed under State law RCW 29A.68.020, the court pointed out that previous cases in the State Supreme Court, most notably *Foulkes v. Hays*, 85 Wn. 2d 629, had recognized that election contests could also be maintained under RCW 29A. 68.011.

The court also ruled there were two exemptions to the timing of voter registration challenges—if more than one vote is cast by a single voter, or a vote is cast by a felon or someone declared mentally incompetent.

On February 4, Bridges announced that the party challenging the election must deliver to the opposite party "a written list of the number of illegal votes and by whom given that the contesting party intends to prove at trial. No testimony may be received as to any illegal votes except as to such as are specified in the list."[30]

Judge Bridges also critically defined the Republicans' ultimate burden of proof.

"With respect to 29A.68.110," the judge said, "no election may be set aside on account of illegal votes unless it appears that an amount of illegal votes has been given to the person whose right is being contested, that, if taken from that person, would reduce the number of the person's legal votes below the number of votes given to some other person for the same office, after deducting there from the illegal votes that may be shown to have been given to the other person."[31]

In other words, Republicans would have to show that Rossi received more valid votes for the Office of Governor than Gregoire.

"I think that's going to be an extraordinarily difficult thing to do," said Democratic Attorney Kevin Hamilton.[32]

"I think they are absolutely wrong," reacted Republican Attorney Diane Tebelius. "There is no doubt in my mind that we are going to have the evidence. We are going to have the proof."[33]

Judge Bridges maintained that Republicans could introduce this key evidence, which might nullify the election, but he also noted that "it may be problematical for the petitioners to ultimately prevail."[34]

No Revote Election

But the Democrats also had reason to celebrate. Their win came when Judge Bridges took a revote off the table.

"No revote in the governor's race. A Judge in Wenatchee has rejected the Republicans' ultimate remedy for the contested gubernatorial election," broadcasted KIRO Radio.[35]

The Republicans had wanted the court to order a revote, while the Democrats argued the court had no such authority. The verdict was critical.

Foulkes v. Hayes

The Republicans hung their hopes on a three-decade-old court case in which a "smoking gun" nullified an election. In this case, the successful challenger did not show which voters had cast illegal votes or how their ballots changed the outcome of the election.

In 1975, Foulkes and Hayes ran for Adams County Commissioner. In the original count, Foulkes claimed the office by just 37 votes out of 3,025 cast. However, in the recount, the tables turned, with Hays winning by 71 votes. Foulkes contested the election and asked the court to set the results aside.

According to Foulkes, someone tampered with votes between election day and the recount because the ballots were not properly secured. They were placed in envelopes, sealed with wax, and locked inside canvass bags with padlocks. However, the keys to the padlocks were tied to the outside of the bags. Although the ballots were then stored in a vault, a number of people had access to the vault.

The State Supreme Court subsequently ruled it could not determine how many ballots had been altered, but nullified the election. The court determined it had authority to allow a revote.

In Chelan County Superior Court, the Republicans would rely heavily on *Foulkes* to convince the court to set the Gregoire election aside, simply because the results were uncertain. The following excerpt provided the heart of the Rossi camp's arguments. (Note that RCW 29.65.010 is now RCW 29A.68.020, and RCW 29.04.030 is now RCW 29A.68.011.)

"Here the trial court correctly ruled that RCW 29.65.010 did not apply to respondent Foulkes' claim. The only subsection of that section which is claimed to be applicable is subsection (5), which allows contests to be brought on the basis of 'illegal votes.' But, as the trial court held, the term 'illegal votes' has been held to refer not to fraudulently altered ballots, but to votes 'cast by persons not privileged to vote and votes not entitled to be counted because not cast in the manner provided by law.' Such a limited interpretation of this phrase here is especially appropriate in light of RCW 29.65.090, which requires a person alleging illegal voting in a statutory election contest to provide the Court with the names of those who cast them. In a situation such as the trial court found existed here, it might be impossible to show by whom the ballots were altered, though it is proven that the alteration took place. To impose a requirement that an election contestant produce a 'smoking gun' to obtain relief in such circumstances would deprive him of relief despite the clear merits of his claim that the election was invalid. RCW 29.65.010 therefore did not apply, and the trial court correctly proceeded under the alternative authority provided it by RCW 29.04.030."[1]

---

1. *Foulkes v. Hays*, 85 Wn.2d 629, 537 P.2d 777 (1975).

Most felt the burden of proof required of the Republicans would be much higher if the court did not have the option of calling for a new election.

Specifically, the Democrats had argued:

- The constitution contained mandatory requirements for the manner in which the Governor is to be elected.
- Nowhere was there any reference or authority for a special election.
- The constitution provided that the Governor was to be elected at the same time as the members of the State legislature, and the next legislative elections were not scheduled until November 2006.

Additionally, they cited numerous other constitutional provisions, which established the principle that no special election for Governor could be held.

They also argued that the election contest statutes themselves did not permit a new election. In their view, the statutes only permitted a court to "declare a person duly elected. What they do not do, implicitly or explicitly, is permit a Court to engage the machinery of the Executive and Legislative branches by ordering a new election to take place."[36]

Briefly, the Republicans argued:

- This motion was premature.
- Clearly the court (as stated in the *Foulkes* case) did have authority to order a new election when a victor was in doubt.

Meanwhile, Reed was deeply concerned about there being a court-appointed Governor. He argued that if the court "eventually concludes that the election results should be set aside, under the law, the voters, and not this Court or the Legislature, would select Washington's governor."[37] If the court "set the election aside," that is, nullified the first election, but did not order a second election, then "a new election would occur under the terms of Article III, Section 10 of the state constitution. That section provides that upon removal of the governor, the duties of office devolve upon the lieutenant governor."[38] The brief further explained that under the constitutional provision, the Lieutenant Governor would continue the duties as Governor only until a "governor shall be elected and qualified."[39]

Nevertheless, Judge Bridges had proceeded to remove a new election as a possible remedy. While acknowledging that some might view this ruling as premature, Bridges disagreed. He pointed out that proofs were not going to change what remedies may be available to the court, and therefore ruling on this motion would not be affected by any evidence introduced later.

The contest case would now decide whether the election of Chris Gregoire as Governor would stand.

The court, which had relied on the *Foulkes* case for a number of its rulings on previous motions, here drew a distinction. "In the *Foulkes* case our Supreme Court was faced with the prospect of addressing the election of a county commissioner. And here, this Court is faced with a state executive officer and there are certain constitutional provisions that attach to a state executive officer."[40]

The court relied heavily on the constitutional provisions cited in the Democrats' motion, specifically those contained in Article III, Section 10.

Bridges concluded: "The petitioners request for—to order, if they're successful, a statewide special election is not permitted by Washington's election contest statute, RCW 29A.68.050... and, more particularly, not permitted by the Washington State Constitution. The Court notes that back in 1902 when we had a vacancy in the governor's office, our Supreme Court looked to the constitution, not the Court's inherent powers to resolve how that vacancy was to be dealt with as far as elections were concerned. And so, in response to the intervenor's motion, I'm going to grant the motion and the Court's going to strike that portion of the petition which requests what I call special relief, that is, the Court order a new election. The Court doesn't have that authority either under the statute, or the Constitution, and the Court thinks it should not exercise it on grounds of equity."[41]

Subject Matter Jurisdiction

The Democrats also argued that the court had no jurisdiction in election contests involving the Governor, and that the decision rested with the legislature. The "Washington Constitution vests that power exclusively in the Legislature."

The constitutional language relied upon by the Democrats said that contested elections for the Governor "shall be decided by the legislature in such manner as shall be determined by law. WASH. CONST., Art. III, Sec. 4."[42]

They asserted: "Washington's statutory election contest provisions...do not give this Court jurisdiction over this matter...the Constitution entrusts election contests for statewide office to the Legislature...the election contest statutes cannot be construed to apply to contests arising out of elections for these officers."[43]

Both the Republicans and Secretary Reed disagreed. They argued:

- The constitution clearly gave the legislature authority to enact laws to govern how such contests were to proceed.
- And, the legislature had clearly done so in the election contest statute giving the authority to the court.

Secretary Reed's brief specifically cited amendments to the election contest statutes in 1977. "Before 1977, the Legislature withheld jurisdiction from the courts concerning contested elections involving the state executive branch."[44]

"The Washington Legislature decided in 1977 to extend our State's election contest statute to broadly provide for court proceedings in all election contests [instead of just county, district, and precinct contests]. That 1977 expansion is fatal to the Democrat's statutory claim, for the manner provided for in that enactment does not in any way purport to withhold from the court's jurisdiction over election contests that happen to involve a statewide office such as the Governor."[45]

The Court's Ruling

Judge Bridges ruled the courts did have subject matter jurisdiction.

"Article III, Section 4 conferred upon the legislature the authority to delegate the hearing of election contests and that, in 1977 and thereafter, the legislature enacted an election contest statute conferring jurisdiction to hear all election contests upon those persons named in RCW 29A.68.011, which include again justices of the Supreme Court, judges of the Court of Appeals, and judges of the Superior Court in the proper county."[46]

Thus, the disputed 2004 Governor election would be resolved by the court and not the legislature.

Improper Venue

The Democrats charged that Chelan County Superior Court was not the proper venue for an election contest case filed against every county election officer and the State's chief election officer. They argued:

- Under the provisions of RCW 29A.68.011, the Washington State Supreme Court was the appropriate court for the contest case.
- If the Chelan Court and the Supreme Court were both proper, the contest should be transferred to the Supreme Court for convenience.
- If the case was not transferred to the Supreme Court, it should be transferred to the Thurston County Superior Court—the appropriate court because that was where the certificate of election was issued, where the rules and procedures for conducting the election and the recounts were developed, and where the Chief Election Officer resided.

"This court [the Chelan County Superior Court] is not the 'appropriate' court under these statutes for this election contest," they argued. "A superior court could, of course, be the proper forum for some election contests, such as contests challenging elections for county or city officers. Here, however, Petitioners challenge the election for a statewide official—an election conducted under the oversight of a statewide official—and name all the counties and chief election officials of the state as respondents."[47]

They concluded that because of the relief asked for by the petitioners, which was the removal of a sitting Governor, "a superior court is not the 'appropriate' court to issue such an order."[48]

Both the Republicans and Secretary Reed disagreed. The Republicans argued:

- The Superior Court of Chelan County was an "appropriate" venue for the case.
- One of the respondents was Chelan County.
- Much of the legal work had already been done with the understanding that Chelan County would be the venue, and that the statute clearly gave the superior court jurisdiction.[49]
- The election contest statute recognizes that such contests often require fact-finding and

supervision of discovery, for which the State Supreme Court is ill-equipped.[50]

The Court's Ruling

The court denied the Democrats' motion. Judge Bridges in his oral ruling pointed out that "our courts have held that venue statutes should be read together such that a suit against multiple counties or county officials can be brought where venue is proper as to any one of those persons or entities. Chelan County is such a county because both the county as well as its auditor have been named as defendants in this case…this judge has concurrent jurisdiction with any other of the 176 judges of the Superior courts…or 22 judges of the Courts of Appeals or the nine justices of the Supreme court."[51]

A number of counties had argued they ought to be dismissed from the case since no specific allegations had been made against them. Judge Bridges decided not to rule on the individual motions from counties, but rather, perhaps surprisingly, dismissed all of the counties and county auditors from the case.

"I don't see where the counties—and this is not a criticism of the cluster of prosecutors that we actually have here…—I can't see where…the counties' participation is necessarily helpful to the Court and probably in the administration of justice or the efficient administration of justice, they're not necessarily helpful and are more burdensome.

"I don't read the election contest statute as requiring the counties…I think discovery can proceed whether the counties are in or they're out. In other words, I don't see any prejudice to petitioners in dismissing the counties from this action. Now…there may be folks who would like to stay in this action and that's certainly welcome, I'm sure, by everybody and they can do that, but they need to indicate that affirmatively, that they intend to stay in."[52]

In a few moments, Judge Bridges reduced the number of respondents in the case by 78. Unless they chose to remain, all counties and county auditors were now dismissed from the case.

Therefore, the critical hearing on February 4 concluded, sending the 2004 Governor election to trial.

"This was a crushing day for the Democrats," said Rossi spokeswoman Mary Lane. "Our case is moving forward, and I think they're just grasping for anything."[53]

"We're dancing and they're crying," said Republican attorney Mark Braden. "I didn't hear us lose anything."[54]

However, Democrats prevailed on two counts. First, the option of a revote had disappeared, and any statewide citizens' campaign for a second election was legally meaningless. (By this date, political consultant Sharon Gilpin had provided the legislature with petitions, and claimed to have acquired the signatures of 241,000 voters supporting a revote.)

Second, Republicans were now charged with proving Rossi actually received more valid votes than Gregoire. "The ruling's effect is, they now have to specifically prove that Mr. Rossi won the election," said Democratic Attorney Russ Speidel.[55]

Thus, merely demonstrating that some illegal votes were cast would fall short; the Republicans had to show evidence that the wrong candidate had been allowed to assume duties as Governor.

Endnotes

1. Election contest petition, p. 4.
2. 2004 election coverage, KIRO 710 Newsradio, Bonneville International Corporation.
3. Office of the Secretary of State, "Reed Statement Regarding Contested Election Court Case Filed Today," media statement, January 7, 2005.
4. Election contest petition, pp. 5–7.
5. Motion to intervene, pp. 5–7.
6. Article III, Section 1 provides, in part, as follows: "The executive department shall consist of a governor...who shall be severally chosen by the qualified electors of the state at the same time and place of voting as for members of the legislature."
7. Motion to intervene, p. 1.
8. "Section 1 Executive Department. The executive department shall consist of a governor, lieutenant governor, secretary of state, treasurer, auditor, attorney general, superintendent of public instruction, and a commissioner of public lands, who shall be severally chosen by the qualified electors of the state at the same time and place of voting as for the members of the legislature." Article III, Section 1, Washington State Constitution.
9. David Postman, "GOP Seeks Criminal Records," *Seattle Times*, January 14, 2005.
10. The Snohomish County Council later rescinded the request and it was subsequently withdrawn by the prosecuting attorney's office.
11. David Postman, "GOP Loses Round in Election Case," *Seattle Times*, January 21, 2005.
12. Ibid.
13. Neil Modie, "GOP Loses Request to Speed Up Court Case Seeking Revote for Governor," *Post-Intelligencer*, January 21, 2005.
14. Ibid.
15. Ibid.
16. "Scores of Felons Voted Illegally," *Seattle Times*, January 23, 2005.
17. Ibid.
18. In late March 2006, a King County Superior Court declared that the requirement for full payment of all financial requirements violated the Equal Protection clause of the U.S. Constitution because of its impact on indigent felons.
19. "Scores of Felons Voted Illegally," *Seattle Times*, January 23, 2005.
20. David Postman, "GOP Says It Found 300 Illegal Votes," *Seattle Times*, January 27, 2005.
21. Ibid.
22. Ibid.
23. David Postman, "Judge Might Void Election, Won't Order New One," *Seattle Times*, February 5, 2005.
24. David Postman, "Rossi Declares Himself Winner in Latest Round of Court Fight," *Seattle Times*, February 8, 2005.
25. "Reply in Support of WSDCC's [Washington State Democratic Central

Committee] Motion to Dismiss Causes for Election Contest," p. 1.
26. Ibid., p. 2.
27. Ibid., pp. 3–4.
28. Secretary of State's response to "WSDCC's Motion to Dismiss Causes Election Contest," p. 2.
29. Ibid.
30. Ibid., p. 22.
31. 2004 election coverage, KIRO 710 Newsradio, Bonneville International Corporation.
32. Ibid.
33. Ibid.
34. Ibid.
35. 2004 election coverage, KIRO 710 Newsradio, Bonneville International Corporation.
36. "Washington State Democratic Central Committee's [WSDCC] Motion to Strike Petitioners Requested Relief," p. 8.
37. Secretary of State's response to "WSDCC's Motion to Strike Petitioner's Requested Relief," p. 2.
38. Ibid., pp. 2–3.
39. Ibid., p. 3.
40. Verbatim report of proceedings; court's oral decision, p. 30.
41. Ibid., pp. 31–32.
42. "WSDCC's Motion to Dismiss for Lack of Subject Matter Jurisdiction," p. 2.
43. Ibid.
44. Secretary of State's response to "WSDCC's Motion to Dismiss for Lack of Subject Matter Jurisdiction," p. 5.
45. Ibid.
46. Verbatim report of proceedings; court's oral decision, p. 9.
47. "WSDCC's Motion to Dismiss for Improper Venue or, in the Alternative, to Transfer Venue," p. 5.
48. Ibid.
49. RCW 29A.68.011.
50. "Petitioners' Opposition to the WSDCCs Motion to Dismiss for Improper Venue," p. 4.
51. Verbatim report of proceedings; court's oral decision, pp. 11–12.
52. Ibid., pp. 14–15.
53. Lewis Kamb, "Judge: No Revote in Governor Dispute," *Post-Intelligencer*, February 5, 2005.
54. David Postman, "Judge Might Void Election, Won't Order New One," *Seattle Times*, February 5, 2005.
55. Lewis Kamb, "Judge: No Revote in Governor Dispute," *Post-Intelligencer*, February 5, 2005.

The whole world will change at that point in time, one way or the other. Either we're moving in the right direction or we're not.

Chapter Nine

Ready for Battle

With election day long past and campaign signs gathering dust, the political parties remained energized in preparing for a trial that could ultimately deliver a new governor.

Interviews were scheduled and sworn statements were taken from almost anyone with some stake in the proceedings. The flood of public information requests swamped election offices like never before.

Public announcements and challenges grew more complex. Democrats accused Rossi of stumbling over whether he would welcome a court-declared victory.

"Dino Rossi told the public he wouldn't accept the court installing him as governor, but [yesterday] he went back on his word, then reversed...Rossi is willing to break his promise, but not until he absolutely has to," said Democratic Party spokeswoman Kristin Brost.[1]

* * *

Meanwhile, according to pollster Stuart Elway, public support for the Republican effort to take hold of the Governor's Office was diminishing.

"For a substantial but dwindling number of people, this is a real cause," said Elway. "I think he's [Rossi] right, that most people think he won the election. But even that is fading or being replaced, for some people, with the idea that it's over now, it's history."[2]

Rossi dedicated more time to his wife and four children as the agonizing wait continued.

"Hopefully within a month's time, we'll have a decision by this court," he said. "The whole world will change at that point in time, one way or the other. Either we're moving in the right direction or we're not."[3]

While a stubborn cloud of doubt hovered over the State's chief executive office, newly declared Governor Christine Gregoire announced new cabinet appointments.

Meanwhile, one-time gubernatorial candidate and King County Chief Executive Ron Sims touted what he considered to be a superior election season. Sims issued a special report on the 2004 elections in an effort to educate voters and to improve public opinion of his embattled office.

"In this election season we registered the most voters ever, mailed out the most absentee ballots ever, had one of the highest turnouts ever, received the most absentee ballots ever, and counted them faster then ever before.

"We had a superlative primary that surpassed all expectations. We had an accuracy rate that any bank would envy. And we were open, honest, and transparent every step of the way."[4]

The media, however, sharply criticized Sims' public relations effort.

Meanwhile, the legal preparations for trial continued as Judge Bridges ruled on key motions. Amid confusion over some of the orders, the Democrats, in particular, were eager for Bridges to clarify that Republicans must show both the number of illegal votes *and* for whom those votes were cast.

Claims of Illegal Votes, February 22

During the same time period, more claims of illegal votes materialized.

On February 22, Republicans and the Building Industry Association of Washington (BIAW)[5] claimed to have uncovered the names of 1,108 felons who voted in the November election. They announced that the bulk of those votes, some 884, were cast in King County.

The Democrats wanted the names of the alleged felons, while Republican Attorney Harry Korrell defended the privacy of those on the list and the integrity of the Republicans' investigation.

"It is a very sensitive issue, as you can imagine," Korrell said. "We are 99.999 percent confident that we have this exactly right. But is it possible there's a single mistake on the list of 1,108? Yes, it is."[6]

On March 4, the Republicans publicly released their list, which by this point had grown to 1,135 names.

The Democrats were confident inaccuracies would appear.

"I think we're going to find that most of this is business as usual," said David McDonald, the Democratic Party's chief counsel. "They've done a good job of press releases and superficial checking but not of doing their homework."[7]

Though the Democrats publicly displayed confidence, the party distributed a letter to its members of a much different tone—asserting that one of President Bush's top advisors, Karl Rove, had his hand in the Republican lawsuit.

"Renew your membership today at the most generous level you can afford and help…stop Rove's mignons [sic] in their tracks."[8]

Republicans later acknowledged that the list did in fact include errors. The *Seattle Times* determined that at least 165 of the alleged felons were juveniles, and thus did not have their civil rights taken away.

Meanwhile, a number of the proven illegal voters were pulled from the voting registers. On March 9, following an investigation by the *Seattle Times*, King County Prosecutor Norm Maleng announced that 99 convicted felons believed to have voted in the November election would have their voter registration revoked. According to Maleng, prosecutors would next concentrate on 800 more felons alleged to hold illegal registrations and identified by the Republican Party.

"This is just the first stage of a process that will continue as we receive and investigate allegations of felons who remain on our voter rolls," Maleng said.[9]

But some of the illegally registered voters planned to challenge their revocations. One was a Rossi voter, Paul Walker, imprisoned in 2001 for the possession of methamphetamine.

"They don't tell you anything about those rights. I never knew it was a permanent situation," the 38-year-old Seattle resident said. "I did my time and I think I should be able to come back to society."[10]

The Numbers Mount

Surprises out of King County continued. In mid-March, Elections Director Dean Logan acknowledged before the King County Council that 660 provisional ballots were counted before their voter eligibility was checked.

The ballots were never set aside in order that their qualifications could be verified. Instead, election workers improperly fed them directly through ballot-tabulation machines. There now was no way to segregate them from the almost 900,000 ballots cast in King County.

"It's an area where we have to do better and we will do better," Logan maintained.[11]

More Ballots Found

A couple of weeks later, King County discovered a number of absentee ballots that had never been counted, stunning an already skeptical public.

Republican members of the King County Council called for a federal investigation.

Some called for Logan to step down, but Ron Sims strongly defended him.

"These unopened and uncounted ballots are the result of the systemic problems he is working to fix," Sims said in a prepared statement. "It is important to let him finish the job he has begun."[12]

To the Republicans, these 94 valid absentee ballots opened the door to fraud. They felt that many of the "found" ballots came from Rossi "strongholds" in King County. Many believed this discovery would pay off in court.

"The focus of the trial will be on whether or not we can reliably say who won," said Jay Vander Stoep, an attorney and adviser to Rossi. "On that basis new ballots showing up makes it far easier for the judge to say 'We don't know.'"[13]

Democratic Attorney Hamilton believed the fraud accusation was the latest Republican tactic to nullify the election.

"Now the theory is what? Somehow they went through Rossi precincts and stuffed ballots under the rug so they wouldn't get counted?" he said. "I'm sorry to laugh. But it's so implausible."[14]

Democrats Join Hunt for Illegal Votes

Not to be outdone by their Republican adversaries, Democrats, too, focused on illegal votes. They concentrated their efforts where Rossi prevailed—with a close eye on eastern Washington.

"It is apparent that the Republicans have cherry-picked all over the state in an effort to present a distorted picture to the court," said Kevin Hamilton. "If they want to talk about any category of error, we need to talk about them all over the state."[15]

The Republicans, meanwhile, filed a motion in court to exclude any and all evidence of illegal votes gathered by the Democrats. They argued it was simply too late for them to suddenly introduce new evidence.

"The only errors asserted in this election contest are those pled by Petitioners in their election contest petition," they argued in their April 13 filing. "If the WSDCC [Washington State Democratic Central Committee] intended to raise allegations of error, misconduct, or negligence, it should have filed a responsive pleading answering Petitioners' petition and asserting counterclaims of defenses… The Court should not allow it to pursue claims that have never been."[16]

Pending a ruling from the judge on the Republicans' motion, the Democrats continued their search for illegal felon voters. In early May, they revealed 743 illegal votes in counties carried by Rossi. State Democratic Party Chair Paul Berendt said the discovery confirmed his suspicion that Republicans were aware of the ballots, but had "concealed illegal votes" that had benefited Rossi.[17]

Trial Date Set

On April 4, Judge Bridges set May 23 as the trial date for the election contest. He indicated it would last about two weeks. In doing so, Bridges denied a request by the Democrats that the trial be delayed six months. He said he chose the date in part because of a "nudge" from attorneys representing Secretary Reed, who sided with the Republicans in seeking a quick trial. Thomas Ahearne, representing Reed, had argued: "Fairness to the voters requires this election contest proceeding to be resolved quickly."[18]

Trial Questions Remain, May 2

But a number of critical questions remained regarding the pending court trial.

Would the Republicans be required to show *how* each individual illegal vote was cast—or simply that the number of illegal votes was greater than the margin of victory? Could the Republicans, instead, use a statistical analysis by expert witnesses to show the *likely* effect of illegal votes?

Statistics and Evidence

Secretary Reed supported the Republicans in their attempt to use statistical "proportional analysis" to show how illegal votes may have influenced the outcome of the election.

Republicans argued that if a statistical analysis determined that Rossi *likely* defeated Gregoire, then the 2004 Governor election should be set aside.

The Secretary of State believed the Republican Party ought to have the opportunity to use an apportioned vote argument, and the court could decide its value after weighing the evidence.

The Democrats argued no such statistical analysis was valid, and had never been used by any Washington court to determine vote totals. Therefore, they concluded, such evidence should be prohibited.

Motions before the Court

Both political parties filed a number of motions.

The Democrats argued:

- Non-citizen votes[19] did not constitute illegal votes.
- The Republican motion seeking to clarify the burden of proof for illegal voters—as it related to felon voters—should be denied.
- The issue of "voter crediting" should be excluded from consideration as evidence of illegal voting.
- Evidence of illegal voting by felons should be excluded, unless the Republicans prove it by "clear and convincing evidence," satisfying special criteria for including evidence of how a felon voted.

Additionally, the Republicans argued:

- Any evidence of off-setting errors favoring Dino Rossi that might be submitted by the Democrats should be excluded.

Each party, of course, opposed the motions offered by the other side, whereas the Secretary of State's views were divided. Reed supported the Democrats' motion to exclude evidence of non-citizen voting because, unlike the felon voters, such "voters" did fit into the category defined by State law (RCW 29A.68.020) as "persons who should have been challenged prior to the election."

The Secretary opposed the Republican motion to shift the burden of proof of illegal voters to the Democrats and to the counties accused of making mistakes. The Republicans, on the other hand, had argued that a felon's conviction coupled with the absence of a certificate of discharge was *prima facie* evidence of illegal voting. It was the Secretary's position that the burden of proof rested with the party—the Republicans—contesting the election in the first place.

Reed also maintained that lists of people credited with voting were not a reliable evidence of turnout, arguing:

- Why use crediting to count the number of votes cast when every county had the exact count of voter signatures on envelopes and poll books—and numbers on the canvass certified by the canvassing boards? Empty return envelopes [no ballot inside] were credited for voting [a practice changed by the Washington State Legislature a short time later].

- Why only cast out illegal votes for Gregoire, but not illegal votes for Rossi? The goal of the election contest was to determine the winner by counting all legal votes.

Reed therefore supported the Democrats' position that crediting lists should be excluded as evidence.

On the issue of the Democrats' motion to exclude any person appearing on the list of convicted felons not satisfying special criteria, Reed agreed with the Democrat's criteria, but felt the motion itself was premature.

Finally, Reed opposed the Republican motion to exclude any off-setting errors discovered by the Democrats, arguing: "Allowing evidence of illegal votes and election official misconduct that affected the number of lawful votes counted for the runner up (Mr. Rossi), while excluding evidence of illegal votes and election official misconduct that affected the number of lawful votes counted for the winner (Ms. Gregoire), would only tell half the story. The over 1.3 million voters who voted for Mr. Rossi and the over 1.3 million voters who voted for Ms. Gregoire deserve the whole story—not half."[20]

The Judge Rules

On May 2, Judge Bridges ruled that Republicans could offer evidence showing how illegal votes might have affected the election—by using expert testimony and utilizing a statistical analysis process. But Bridges clarified that the Democrats could challenge the scientific value of any evidence offered.

"However, and this is important," Bridges told the attorneys, "the denial of this [the Democrats'] motion should not be interpreted as a pretrial ruling adopting the statistical analysis methodology."[21]

Bridges denied Republican efforts to exclude any evidence of illegal votes turned up by the Democrats. He stated that since the law dealing with election contests required illegal votes to be subtracted from both candidates, each side should have the opportunity to present evidence regarding such votes.

Further, Bridges ruled that any party alleging illegal votes must show a copy of that voter's signature on either an absentee ballot envelope or in a poll book.

He stated that the number of voters "credited" with voting was not relevant.

Bridges also denied motions from both parties regarding the proof of votes cast by unqualified felons. However, the standard Bridges set was closer to what the Democrats wanted. The parties must present "clear and convincing" evidence he ruled, and establish six standards similar to what the Democrats had proposed—the voter was convicted as an adult, was convicted of a felony, was not given a deferred sentence, has not had his or her voting rights restored, had cast a ballot in the November election, and had voted for a gubernatorial candidate.[22] Finally, he granted the Democrats' motion to exclude evidence of the two non-citizens who voted, ruling that such voters should have been challenged prior to the election.

Thus, although the Republicans won an important victory by the court's approval of statistical analysis, the Democrats also won on several fronts. Any statistical analysis experts presented by the Republicans would be subject to cross-examination by the Democrats, the Democrats' standard of proof had largely been accepted by the court, and the issue of voters "credited" with voting had been dismissed by the court. Additionally, the Democrats could offer their own examples of illegal votes cast for Rossi.

In short, using strict guidelines, the Republicans must show that Rossi received more valid votes than Gregoire. The judge had reaffirmed his earlier ruling that, with no allegations of fraud, it would not be enough to show that the number of illegal votes exceeded Gregoire's margin of victory. Republicans must establish that Gregoire owed her victory to illegal votes.[23]

Secretary Reed Honored for Integrity

A week later, Secretary Reed received an award for his conduct during the controversial election and subsequent recounts. Spokane's Gonzaga Law School granted Reed its highest honor.

Professor Stephen Sepinuck explained at the ceremony, "Sam Reed has shown exemplary character and legal judgment during the ongoing political maelstrom involving the state's gubernatorial election. In a time when public employees are called bureaucrats and elected officials are merely seen as partisan politicians, Sam Reed demonstrated himself to be the ideal public servant."[24]

Declarations of Fraud

Just days before the trial, Republicans made another claim. In spite of Judge Bridges' ruling on the credited voters issue, Republican Chairman Vance zeroed in on the discrepancies between the number of people credited with voting and the number of ballots actually cast. Vance concluded the discrepancies made it "impossible to rule out the possibility that votes were fraudulently added or subtracted from this election."[25]

Admissions from Nicole Way

To add fuel to the "fraud" fire, the absentee-ballot supervisor in King County, Nicole Way, admitted in a deposition that she falsified a report that all absentee ballots had been accounted for in the November election.

Under oath, Way admitted that she and supervisor Garth Fell never determined how many mail ballots had actually been returned. To compensate, they simply added the number of ballots counted to the number of ballots rejected for a final count.

Way claimed the county's new election management system was unable to provide the figure.

This situation was assessed in a *Seattle Times* editorial:

"Faith in the county's election system is eroded by the fact that Nicole Way…and her boss Garth Fell… prepared a report that failed to use all available information to verify the mail-ballot figures.

"Presenting the report to the Canvassing Board was equal parts bad judgment and lack of skill in using the new county computer system.

"It is important to understand, however, what the action represents and what it does not.

"From what is now known, neither Way nor Fell tried to affect voting or change the outcome of the election. They did not stuff the ballot box or try to turn away voters. None of that.

"The mail-ballot report represents more trouble at county elections but it does not amount to a falsified document, as we understand how things transpired. The state Republican Party Web site proclaims King County elections officials admit fraud. They do not.

"From the information currently available, this action, embarrassing, sloppy and indefensible as it is, does not rise to that level."[26]

On the eve of the trial, the *Times* ran a comprehensive story on felon voting and applied a statistical analysis similar to the method to be used in court. The *Times* applied the methodology to both of the party's lists of felons—the Republican list of 964 felon voters, and the Democratic list of 794. The newspaper concluded that even with the apportioned voting method, Christine Gregoire won the election.

The article also emphasized that both lists were heavily partisan in nature. On the Republican list, 75 percent of the alleged felon voters came from precincts Gregoire carried, while the Democrats' list focused on precincts Rossi carried.

Republican Chairman Vance remained optimistic.

"We think we win on either illegal votes or neglect, fraud, mistakes, errors, whatever you want to call it. We think we win either way."[27]

Voters across the state would soon find out.

Endnotes

1. Neil Modie, "To Be, or Not to Be, Governor," *Post-Intelligencer*, February 8, 2005.
2. Rich Roesler, "Governor-in-waiting Waits on Court; Rossi Has Confidence in Revote Case, but Time May Not Be on His Side," *Spokesman-Review*, February 16, 2005.
3. Ibid.
4. King County Executive, www.metrokc.gov, February 9, 2005.
5. Tactics used by the BIAW were extensively criticized by Democrats and the media. BIAW sent admittedly phony housing surveys to more than 400 voters who had signed absentee and provisional ballot affidavits, offering a $10 check to those who returned the survey. BIAW then compared signatures on the "surveys" with signatures on the ballot affidavits in an attempt to prove fraud. The *Seattle Times*, in a March 8, 2005, editorial, called the tactic "political sleaze."
6. David Postman and Jonathan Martin, "GOP Mum on Felon-voter Names," *Seattle Times*, February 24, 2005.
7. "Rossi Team Issues List of 'Felon' Voters," *Seattle Times*, March 4, 2005.
8. David Postman. "Democratic Chief Says Rove Lurks behind GOP Suit," *Seattle Times*, March 5, 2005.
9. Mike Carter, "Voter-list Purges Targets 99 Felons," *Seattle Times*, March 9, 2005.
10. Ibid.
11. Keith Ervin, "Tally of Mishandled Ballots Grows," *Seattle Times*, March 15, 2005.
12. Keith Ervin, "Republicans Request Investigation in Governor's Race," *Seattle Times*, April 4, 2005.
13. David Postman, "Latest Vote Snafu Alters Focus of Election Fight," *Seattle Times*, April 10, 2005.
14. Ibid.
15. David Postman, "Democrats Search for Errors in GOP Land," *Seattle Times*, April 10, 2005.
16. "Petitioners' Motion in Limine to Exclude Resurrected or Rehabilitated Provisional Ballots," pp. 7–8, April 13, 2005.
17. Gregory Roberts, "Democrats List 743 Felon Votes as Illegal," *Post-Intelligencer*, May 7, 2005.
18. David Postman, "May 23 Trial Set for Rossi Lawsuit," *Seattle Times*, April 6, 2005.
19. The Republicans identified two allegedly illegal votes cast by non-citizens.
20. "As to the Democrats' Argument to Exclude…"
21. Judge John Bridges, Ibid.
22. Ibid.
23. Gregory Roberts, "GOP Wins Key Issue, Keeps Alive Vote Suit," *Post-Intelligencer*, May 3, 2005.
24. Professor Stephen Sepinuck, Gonzaga Law School, May 10, 2005.
25. David Postman, "GOP Says November Election Tainted by Fraud," *Seattle Times*, May 18, 2005.
26. "Bad Judgment, Errors in County Elections," *Seattle Times*, May 21, 2005.
27. "Toss Out Felon Vote, Gregoire Still Wins," *Seattle Times*, May 23, 2005.

The question is what does our election statute as currently written require.

Chapter Ten

The Trial

Wenatchee is a scenic, charming town located next to the eastern foothills of the Cascade Range. Orchards stretch across much of the valley, producing the famous Washington apples that earned the city its nickname, the Apple Capital of the World.

On Monday, May 23, media, satellite trucks, and lawyers arrived in the central Washington town for a two-week trial that could ultimately oust the State's sitting chief executive. For this particular moment at least, the Apple Capital received equal billing as host of the legal effort to nullify the election of Governor Christine Gregoire.

Media broadcast the court challenge live.

"I'm Tim Haeck live in Wenatchee, where a long-awaited trial is about to begin."[1]

As the historic trial started, Republican attorney Dale Foreman—once a gubernatorial candidate himself—delivered a daring opening argument.

"This election was stolen from the legal voters of this state by a bizarre combination of illegal voters and bungling bureaucrats," Foreman told the judge.[2]

Foreman used words such as "sinister fraud" and "corruption" in what he described as an election tainted by more than shoddy record keeping. Election workers, he claimed, were not just reckless with absentee ballots in King County; they manipulated votes and "stuffed" ballot boxes.

"Our citizens' right to choose their own Governor was violated by the outrageous and illegal conduct of many people, from those who committed fraud by voting twice, those who committed fraud by casting votes for dead people, nearly 1,000 felons who voted when their right to vote had never been restored, and the elections officials in King County who allowed thousands of illegal votes to be cast and failed to follow the most basic ballot security procedures."[3]

Foreman introduced the courtroom to an inaccurate ballot "report" he claimed linked King County election managers to fraud. The report was supposed to precisely summarize the number of absentee ballots that voters mailed back to King County, but in 2004, the count was flawed. According to staff, the county's new voter registration system was not well equipped to accurately track absentee ballots. The report in question was designed to reconcile the number of absentee ballots returned with the number counted and the number rejected. Each of those numbers should have been traced independently, permitting the form to show whether the votes reconciled. Instead of independently verifying the number of absentee ballots returned, the form was completed by simply adding the number of absentee ballots counted to the number rejected.

"They handed it to the King County Canvassing Board knowing it was a lie, knowing it was fraud," Foreman claimed.[4]

But Democratic Attorney Kevin Hamilton countered this allegation of fraud by calling the Republicans desperate.

"Fraud is not part of this case and it never has been. Obviously, there is some desperation seeping into the petitioner's case. Every election has irregularities. They occur in every county in this state, in every state in the nation. This democracy of ours is not a perfect system, and we all recognize that."[5]

According to Hamilton, Republicans had no hard evidence. Despite an army of lawyers statewide watching the counts, Hamilton said the Republican Party had failed to depose a single poll worker.

"If someone sneezed they saw it, but not one of them will be called to testify in this trial," he said.[6]

The partisan wrangling before the court was openly acknowledged by Assistant Attorney General Jeff Even, representing Secretary of State Sam Reed.

"In a narrow, immediate sense, this election contest is a fight between the Republicans and the Democrats over whose candidate should be Governor."[7]

But Even reminded the judge of Washington's penchant for close races and the broader impact of the court case over time. Even made clear that Secretary Reed would not advocate for either candidate; his sole interests were to ensure a clear, comprehensive account of the Gregoire-Rossi election and recounts, and to protect the integrity of Washington's democracy.

That afternoon, the Republicans began their case. In an unusual approach, Dale Foreman posed as Secretary Reed reading his sworn statements to the court room and even imitating the Secretary's calm, congenial style. Included was Reed's candid description of the situation in King County.

"The organizational culture represented by these people over the years has often been to kind of protect themselves by not letting people at higher levels know about mistakes and problems. And in elections, you want them to have the opposite attitude. It is imperative that as soon as they discover a problem that they report it upward."[8]

Tuesday, May 24—Day Two

On the morning of May 24, the Republican strategy focused on Chelan County Auditor Evelyn Arnold, who supervised a clean General Election in rural central Washington. Republicans hoped her testimony would sharply contrast with the occurrences in metropolitan King County.

Foreman: If you had reason to believe as the county auditor that your votes did not reconcile, would you knowingly send the Secretary of State a form that said they did reconcile?

Arnold: No I would not.

Foreman: As both a CPA and an auditor, why would you not do that?

Arnold: Well, the numbers—I believe that that would come out. I just couldn't do that. Numbers need to reconcile. We end up with recounts. Things will come out eventually. So you need to be forthright at the very beginning. And that's how you find your answers, is by being forthright.[9]

The Republican witness testified on county procedures designed to prevent double voting, provisional ballot problems, and mistakes on ballot reconciliation reports—the kinds of errors that showed up in King County.

But in the cross-examination, Democrat Attorney Jenny Durkan contrasted rural Chelan County, handling fewer than 30,000 votes, 80 precincts, and 7 polling places, with a large metropolitan county. In King County, 900,000 voters cast ballots from 2,616 precincts and 540 polling places. King was the 12th largest county in the nation. Elections there were, without argument, an enormous undertaking. And, as Chelan County's auditor conceded, far more complex.

On the witness stand, Arnold also admitted that, in spite of their best efforts, eight felons voted in Chelan County.

Durkan: Is it a mistake or error to count votes cast by a felon whose civil rights have not been restored?

Arnold: Yes, it is.

Durkan: Did Chelan County in your knowledge count felon votes in the 2004 General Election?

Arnold: I found out afterward that we did.[10]

Republicans next called the King County Superintendent of Elections, Bill Huennekens, to the witness stand. As a manager, Huennekens was key to the fraud allegation. Republicans said Huennekens was well aware of the problems with the absentee ballot report.

"His deputy, Garth Fell, said in a sworn deposition that Huennekens knew the details beforehand,"[11] wrote David Postman, the *Seattle Times* chief political reporter.

Under oath, Huennekens admitted that no exact count of absentee ballots cast in the race existed. But he denied any involvement with the report. Huennekens acknowledged providing the canvassing board with the final summary, but clarified that he did not prepare the totals or know how those figures were reached.

Republican Attorney Robert Maguire asked about King County ballots turning up weeks and even months after election day.

Maguire: Since the November 2004 Election, has King County found any uncounted, valid absentee ballot from that election?

Huennekens: Yes.

Maguire: How many?

Huennekens: 96 I believe.

Maguire: When were they found?

Huennekens: They were found over a period of time, a week or so, in our effort to comply with discovery requests.

Maguire: In response to discovery requests in the election contest, King County did something that led to finding these ballots?

Huennekens: Correct.

Maguire: What did King County do?

Huennekens: You asked for copies of absentee ballot envelopes with signatures on them from a large number of individuals and we had to go into the archive boxes of ballots and retrieve those. And in doing that, staff found ballots that—envelopes with ballots still in them.[12]

In his cross-examination, Democratic Attorney Kevin Hamilton attempted to demonstrate that all elections are messy, and perfection is nearly impossible to achieve in counties as large as King County. In Hamilton's line of questioning, Huennekens testified that he did not know whether any of the alleged illegal voters influenced the selection of the Governor.

Wednesday, May 25—Day Three

For Republicans, one of the most anticipated witnesses called during the trial was Nicole Way, the King County elections worker pulled into the heart of the controversy after admitting to falsifying the now infamous absentee ballot report.

In King County, she held the position of mail ballot supervisor. As one of two people responsible for the flawed summary, she was questioned extensively.

The Associated Press reported: "On Wednesday, Nicole Way, King County mail ballot supervisor, testified she repeatedly told her bosses as early as spring 2004 that the county elections department could not tell how many ballots were being mailed out or received back. About two-thirds of the county's 900,000 votes in the November election were mail ballots."[13]

"It was as accurate as it could be," Way told Democratic Attorney Jenny Durkan under cross-examination. "I was concerned it was wrong, but I didn't know there were ballots unaccounted for in this report until the 95 were found."[14]

Once the attorneys had finished in court, Judge Bridges had questions of his own for Way.

""Do you have any sense in your mind as you sit here this afternoon that that number is accurate or not?" Bridges asked about the report.

"I don't know," Way said."[15]

"Certainly what she did made it possible for people to commit fraud," Republican Attorney Braden would say after court concluded later that day. "I cannot point to anybody who committed fraud. We're just saying the opportunity was there and it looks suspicious."[16]

"They don't have any evidence of anything," argued Democratic Attorney Hamilton. "Saying there were accounting lapses that could have allowed something to happen is not clear and convincing evidence that anything happened."[17]

Thursday, May 26—Day Four

As is often the case with big, continuing news stories, additional key players in the 2004 election saga had quickly became household names. This was quite evident on day four of the trial, when Elections Director Nick Handy agreed to take part in an online chat with voters via the capitol newspaper, the *Olympian*.

[This is] Kevin [in] Lacey: How come you and [King County's] Dean Logan are still in charge of elections in this state after the total debacle in November? The fraud and/or incompetent actions of election workers is totally unacceptable. Heads need to roll because of this, and it should start at the top. The citizens of Washington State deserve better than this. Any self-respecting person would have resigned their office after reviewing what happened this last election.

Handy: I understand Kevin's perspective and that point of view is held by many people in the state who are very frustrated by the disclosures after the election that have caused uncertainty to rise…I think it's fair to say both Dean [Logan] and I are working as hard as we can to address the problems and bring about reforms to ensure [these problems] don't happen in the future or the occurrence is minimized.[18]

100 Votes

Meanwhile in court, dueling scientists appeared on the witness stand. They attempted to support or debunk a scientific theory, supported by the Republicans, claiming to give Rossi the Governor's office by 100 votes.

The Republican Party's star witness was Jonathan Katz, a political science professor at the California Institute of Technology. Katz applied what is called proportional deduction to the Republicans' list of 1,183 felon voters. His conclusion—Washington's top statewide office belonged to Dino Rossi by a razor-thin margin of just 100 votes.

Katz arrived at his conclusion using proportional deduction and geography—in this case, focusing on a precinct in which each felon voter lived. Following Katz's line of thinking, if a precinct voted 60–40 for Gregoire, and there were 10 felons who voted illegally in that precinct, then 6 votes ought to be subtracted from Gregoire and 4 votes from Rossi. (On the Republicans' list of 1,183 illegal votes, most were cast in King County.)

Both Katz and another witness, Anthony Gill, an associate professor of political science at the University of Washington, testified that proportional deduction was the best way to estimate the number of illegal votes for each candidate.

But in cross-examination, it came out that geography alone fell short. Other factors, such as age or gender, could also be used as criteria for proportional reduction. Or better yet, proportional reduction could be dispensed with altogether by simply asking the felons how they voted.

To rebut the Katz-Gill analysis, the Democrats depended on Christopher Adolph, another assistant professor of political science at the University of Washington and a former graduate assistant to Katz. According to Adolph, statisticians rejected Katz's method.

To illustrate his point, Adolph offered an example: Because the Seattle Mariners as a team batted .270 during the 2004 season, and Ichiro Suzuki was a Seattle Mariner, he too must have batted .270. In fact his average was .372, the best in the American League.

Adolph also testified that Katz's work was flawed because the illegal votes he used did not constitute a scientifically valid sample of all illegal votes cast in the state.

Democrats argued that Republicans "cherry-picked" Democratic precincts in King County to give the most favorable outcome to Rossi.

The Secretary of State attorneys, on their part, argued that the Republicans' expert should testify and his evidence be entered. But, they clarified, the analysis should be evaluated on its merits.

The court appeared undecided on whether proportional deduction was a valid means of determining the true election result, or just junk science.

Katz's testimony resulted in a Frye Hearing, a special court session that would allow the judge to exclude certain scientific testimony if, in his opinion, it did not follow accepted scientific methods.

At the conclusion of the Frye Hearing, Judge Bridges allowed the testimony of Professor Katz and Professor Gill, but with reservations. Bridges said he had concerns about the value of proportional deduction, but would decide later whether to accept it.

Friday, May 27—Day Five

Proportional deduction did not score well with columnist Danny Westneat of the *Seattle Times*, who had sharp words for Republicans the next morning.

"Their fraud claim, supposedly based on statistical science, wouldn't earn a passing grade on the 10th-grade WASL.

"GOP lawyer Dale Foreman told me earlier this week that when I saw the circumstantial evidence of fraud, there would be no doubt in my mind that 'somebody was messing with the ballots.'

"Now that I've seen the evidence, there's no doubt in my mind Republicans ought to be ashamed of themselves."[19]

After submitting more evidence of six people who double voted, plus entering into evidence poll worker descriptions of the difficulty in reconciling ballots, Republicans rested their case. It is worth noting that the Republicans did not call one alleged illegal voter to the stand or submit an affidavit from such a voter into evidence.

Immediately, the Democrats moved for dismissal, arguing that the Republicans had failed to prove anything.

Hamilton: Your Honor, pursuant to Civil Rule 41(b) (3), the Washington State Democrats move to dismiss this election contest.[20]

But the Republicans emphatically denied the accusation, saying that they had identified 789 illegal votes from felons, double voters, and ballots cast in the name of dead people, and that King County's mishandling of provisional ballots also resulted in illegal votes.

They also told Judge Bridges that he was wrong in ruling that they would have to prove Rossi actually won the election. They argued that, under the court case *Foulkes v. Hays*, they only had to show an inability to determine the winner.

The Office of the Secretary of State supported the Republicans in arguing for the case to proceed and be decided on a complete record.

Judge Bridges denied the Democrat's motion to dismiss, saying that both sides deserved "a full and complete analysis, not only of the court's finding of fact but as to the court's conclusions of law."[21]

Bridges also indicated that he wanted to compile as thorough a record as possible for an "inevitable" review by the State Supreme Court.

The Democrats began their case by calling on county auditors, such as Clark County's Greg Kimsey and Spokane's Vicky Dalton, to demonstrate to the court that errors occurred across the state. They argued mistakes that may have benefited Gregoire in King County could have worked to the advantage of Rossi in other counties.

Tuesday, May 31—Day Six
Cheerleader for the Auditors

Some of the liveliest moments of the entire trial occurred on May 31 during the cross-examination of Elections Director Nick Handy.

Hostile questions from Republican Attorney Dale Foreman shocked nearly all observers.

Foreman immediately attacked Handy's impartiality. He accused Handy—who was appointed Elections Director by Republican Reed, worked for three other Republican officials, and ran for statewide office himself as a Republican—of favoring the Democrats.

The accusations centered on an email Handy sent to Attorney Tom Ahearne in January 2005. In the email, Handy commented on the Republicans' charge that the election was fraudulent because of a discrepancy between the number of people credited with voting and the number of ballots actually cast. Handy considered the charge baseless.

Foreman: Here's how you ended this memo, sir. "I expect this will be a major issue raised by the Republicans as they have built their entire public affairs campaign ('every vote should have a voter') around this theme and have worked it hard. If we can successfully demonstrate that this is an unfounded claim, I would hope that this would severely undermine the confidence of the court in the other R claims. Good luck. Nick."

You're neutral in this case?

Handy: Yes, I am.

Foreman: You're neutral in this case?

Handy: Yes, I am.

Foreman: You want to severely undermine the confidence of this honorable Court in our claims regardless of the truth of those claims just because you disagree with us on the crediting issue?

Handy: There are some claims that I believe have been pursued by the Republicans that I do not believe are valid claims. And to the extent that—and this was a classic one. I felt that the Republicans and their public affairs campaign were manipulating information to convince the public that the—of a loss of trust and confidence in the election system. And I felt very strongly that it was a very misleading campaign. I felt very strongly that the information was not correct or accurate. And to the extent that—I did want to have this particular issue essentially exposed. I was very interested in that. I thought that this would really undermine the trust and confidence of the average voter in the elections system in a way that was not fair or accurate. And I believe that today. And I feel just as strongly that our office has maintained as fair and impartial a position in this case as we possibly could.

Foreman: How can you say that?

Handy: I believe that.

Foreman: You're under oath.

Handy: I believe that.

Jenny Durkan: Your Honor, I'm going to object. It's argumentative.

At one point during the cross-examination, Foreman criticized Handy for not reacting sternly to Grays County Auditor Vern Spatz, who admittedly made mistakes.

Foreman: You don't tell him, "Vern, this is a serious matter."

Handy: That's true.

Foreman: "Vern, you made a mistake. Vern, you may have violated the law." You say, "Vern, you are a scholar and a gentleman. Thank you for this most thoughtful note and the recognition for Paul Miller. We appreciate all your good work to ensure that Grays Harbor is correctly processing this election." Aren't you the cheerleader of the state auditors?

Handy: That's your terminology, not mine.[22]

In his questioning of Handy, Secretary of State Attorney Tom Ahearne led him through a number of instances in which the Office of the Secretary of State had opposed the Democrats and supported the Republicans. These included one State Supreme Court case and numerous motions.

Ahearne also pointed out two claims Handy considered invalid—

delayed ballots to the military, and tampering with ballots during duplication and enhancement—which had not survived in the lawsuit. In Ahearne's opinion, this proved Handy was right.

Outside the courtroom, Foreman did not mince words, accusing the Office of the Secretary of State of "masquerading as a neutral party."[23]

This resentment toward the Secretary of State's Office surprised few. Some in the Republican camp felt that because Secretary Reed was a Republican, he should simply fall into lock-step with the party during litigation. Because Reed had sided with both political parties at various times, many Republicans developed hard feelings toward him.

Within the Office of the Secretary of State, Reed had made it abundantly clear his litigation team was to follow the law, announce election procedures, and at all costs avoid getting immersed in partisan rhetoric advanced by either side.

But after court recessed, Republican Attorney Dale Foreman offered a different explanation, pointing out that Judge Bridges looked to the Secretary of State attorneys Tom Ahearne and Jeff Even, "because he thinks they're neutral. I wanted to turn that around and say 'you're not neutral.' We thought it was time to call a spade a spade."[24]

The media had noticed that Secretary Reed's legal team was influential with Bridges, and the judge had acknowledged as much from the bench. But, as David Postman of the *Seattle Times* noted: "Ahearne and Even have presented arguments on both sides of the case. On Friday, Ahearne argued against a Democratic motion to dismiss the case, citing the importance of developing a full record of evidence for an expected appeal. When Bridges ruled against the motion, he mentioned Ahearne's argument."[25]

I Think That's What We're Here to Find Out

In an effort to show mistakes occurred in other counties, the Democrats next called Snohomish County Auditor Bob Terwilliger. Terwilliger described his own problems with a number of ballots, and testified that the likelihood of mistakes increased dramatically in larger counties.

Terwilliger was followed by John Pearson, the Deputy Director of Elections for the Secretary of State's Office. Under cross-examination by Foreman, Pearson was asked whether administrative errors affected the outcome of the Governor's race. He replied, "I think that's what we're here to find out."[26]

Wednesday, June 1—Day Seven Is There Any Sense of Urgency?

The man who many felt owned the bulk of the problems in King County was Dean Logan, Manager of Records, Elections, and Licensing Services. Logan was widely respected in the elections community. He was the first witness for the Democrats on day seven of the trial. Under questioning from Kevin Hamilton, Logan stated that he had been recruited to the position by King County Executive Ron Sims following errors and controversy surrounding the 2002 election.

Logan acknowledged mistakes and difficulties with the county's voter registration systems, but said that without it, the trial would have focused on people who never received their absentee ballots and were denied the right to vote. Logan testified that problems would have been much worse had the county tried to survive another major election without the new system.

In conclusion, Hamilton asked if there was any indication that either Gregoire or Rossi had any involvement in the mistakes or errors discovered during the 2004 election. According to Logan, there was no such indication.

Rob Maguire cross-examined for the Republicans, detailing each mistake documented in King County. Maguire led the courtroom through the typical logistics of the elections process to show opportunities for fraud.

In attempting to open the door to the question of ballot tampering, he specifically focused on the transportation of ballots from post offices to the county facility.

Judge Bridges himself stepped in to ask questions. He read aloud a quote from Logan, who said though problems did occur, they had been addressed "without compromising the transparency or integrity of the election." Bridges appeared to be at best skeptical about this claim, and mentioned that when he had served in the Army, there was an expression about "taking names…and kicking tush."

"Is there any sense of urgency in King County about fixing some of these problems?" he asked Logan.[27] Logan replied that there was and that steps were being taken to address them.

It Is Impossible to Do That

Democrats again called UW Professor Christopher Adolph to the witness stand to try to poke holes in the Republicans' statistical analysis of illegal voters. Adolph said that there was a reason why this method was not used in the social sciences—it just didn't work. He stated once again that the method employed by the Republicans suffered from what statisticians called the "ecological fallacy"—that the behavior of individuals can be inferred from the behavior of the group to which they belong.[28]

Cross-examination of Adolph by Republican Attorney Mark Braden proved contentious at times, both with the witness and with opposing counsel, until finally Judge Bridges asked if perhaps the attorneys needed a break to "contemplate the meaning of things in life."[29] The attorneys apologized, and said they did not need a time out. Braden did get Adolph to concede, however, that it was impossible to know whether Gregoire actually got the most legal votes in the November election.

Braden asked if it was possible to determine if Gregoire was validly elected.

"From the aggregate data, it is impossible to do that," Adolph replied.[30]

Thursday, June 2—Day Eight Confusion over Numbers

Anyone sorting through the mind-boggling statistics and conclusions reported throughout the trial faced plenty of challenges.

On the witness stand, King County Election Operations Supervisor Linda Sanchez described the difficulty in balancing numbers at polling places. She testified that sometimes numbers do not reconcile because of various mistakes.

Noel Frame, who led the Democratic hunt for felon voters, was the next witness called. She supervised a team of about 20 people, who examined some 248,000 absentee ballot envelopes in Pierce County in an effort that resulted in finding 90 potential felon voters.

Under cross-examination, Frame admitted that of the more than 600 felons on their list, all but 11 came from precincts in which Rossi received at least 54 percent of the vote. Harry Korrell asked Frame whether Democrats only searched Rossi precincts. She conceded this was true "because we understood the strong Gregoire precincts had already been researched quite well."[31]

The next witness called, statistics Professor Mark Handcock, claimed that based on the information available to him, Gregoire won the election. Professor Gill, called as a rebuttal witness prior to the Democrats resting their case because of a scheduling conflict, reported that based on the information available to him, Rossi won the election.

Judge Bridges professed confusion over the experts' variations. According to Professor Gill, this was because the experts used differing numbers of illegal votes cast in different areas of the state. His answer seemed to confirm what Judge Bridges had already deduced.

Friday, June 3—Day Nine

On the morning of the last day of the trial, Deputy Elections Director John Pearson took the stand as a rebuttal witness. Pearson was called by the Republicans in an attempt to introduce evidence about an election that had been set aside in Adams County in 1992. Following objections from Jenny Durkan, Judge Bridges ruled such testimony irrelevant and prohibited it from being introduced.

Foreman did question Pearson, however, about the Handy email. Pearson testified that, as a former unit voting officer in the military during a war, he shared some of Handy's frustration and anger over some of the claims made—especially the one regarding military absentee ballots.

The next Republican rebuttal witness was Dan Brady, the party's lead election observer. The Republicans hoped to question Brady about ballot security problems that he had observed. Though Judge Bridges allowed the testimony, he stated that he felt it crossed the line. Over Democratic objections, Bridges allowed the Republicans to continue, saying he was only considering it as rebuttal testimony and not part of the Republican case.

As part of a contentious, and at times hostile, cross-examination of Brady by Kevin Hamilton, the Democrats played a video, over the strenuous objections of the Republicans. The video showed Republican Party Chairman Chris Vance stating that there was no fraud in King County, and "there is nothing nefarious going on in Washington State."[32]

The video was taken at a town hall meeting after the election, but before the recounts when Republicans were clearly more satisfied with the voting process. Under redirect, Brady speculated that Chairman Vance had probably changed his mind and would give a different answer to that question now.

The final witness called in rebuttal was Thurston County Auditor Kim Wyman. The purpose of Wyman's testimony was to again contrast King County's conduct with procedures followed in other counties. The Republicans had begun their case with testimony from a county auditor—Evelyn Arnold—and they were ending it the same way. Dale Foreman paid particular attention to the reconciliation procedures used for both polling place and absentee ballots, and also elicited testimony from Wyman in which she stated she would not submit a report to the canvassing board that she knew was wrong.

Under cross-examination by Hamilton, Wyman admitted to errors that occurred during the Primary in Thurston County, and answered affirmatively when Hamilton asked her if those were the kinds of errors that could happen because of human involvement in the elections process.

The Final Word

Any interest in the election trial that might have faded over the long days of testimony was ramped up again for the closing arguments. Would election mistakes drive a sitting Governor from office? Did someone truly tamper with ballots, as Republicans alleged?

Republican lawyer Harry Korrell, the first to speak, attempted to persuade the judge that Washington voters had been dealt a grave injustice, that the court—through the State's election contest statute—had a clear duty to set aside the results of the 2004 Governor's election and restore public confidence in democracy. Korrell argued that the largest county in the state had no business blaming its serious errors on its size.

"It's not an excuse that King County has more ballots to process. King County has long been the largest, most populous and, I suspect, the wealthiest county in the state. There is no justification for its having what Secretary of State Reed called the most backward elections system in the state and making errors that he called appalling. It is not fair to the voters of the rest of the state to have their votes cancelled out by rampant errors and illegal votes allowed to be counted in King County.

"Your honor, if this contest action fails, this case, an election with the thinnest of margins, where there are far more found ballots than the margin, overwhelming evidence of error and neglect, presented by both sides, ballots that cannot even after seven months be tied to lawful voters. 1,400 felon votes. Votes of dead and double voters. 265 statewide provisional ballots directly into the AccuVote machine outside of King County. 785 in King County alone. Huge discrepancies. Votes counted that appear not to have been cast by lawfully registered voters. And then a disturbing pattern in the distribution of those discrepancies. If this evidence is insufficient in an election decided by 129 votes, then Washington has no meaningful election contest procedure. This cannot be what the Washington Legislature intended.

"Your honor, we recognize the magnitude of what we are asking you to do. But we believe and I think the people of this state believe, that the only way to restore legitimacy to our elections system and confidence that the people have a governor who really was elected by the majority of legal voters, is for the court to set aside the tainted results of this election."[33]

"When you dig deeper into this data, it begins to look sinister. I think we can be forgiven for thinking that something was rotten in King County in this election."[34]

"It simply cannot be that our election contest statute and this court is completely impotent to resolve the staggering problems we have seen in this election."[35]

Finally, Korrell told the court that by applying proportional deduction, the Governor's Office did not belong to Christine Gregoire, but Dino Rossi. The evidence clearly indicated there was more going on than just innocent errors and that fraud was fraud, he argued, whether it was part of some organized effort or the work of individuals.

It Is the Equivalent of the Grassy Knoll

Democratic Attorney Jenny Durkan accused Republicans of failing to offer any evidence of fraud. Instead, she alleged, Republicans chipped away at the public's confidence in democracy with their bogus claims of ballot tampering.

She accused Republican expert witnesses of dressing up a flawed theory as science. She stated that there was no evidence introduced that a single illegal vote was cast for Gregoire, and that the only actual evidence for whom illegal votes had been cast was introduced by the Democrats.[36]

The Democratic attorney added that Republicans were asking the court for staggering relief—throwing out 2.8 million valid votes.

"Our state, like the nation, was deeply divided about the course of our country and our state. But we were not divided about the means of deciding that course. We debate. We protest. We argue. But in the end we vote."[37]

Regarding the Republican claims of detecting a sinister pattern, Durkan said that she had also detected a pattern. Throughout the litigation, she argued, the Republicans had "seized on whatever hot-button issue can cause the most fury regardless of whether they have the facts. In the end, all of these attacks are sound and fury, signifying nothing."[38]

Finally, in a defense of Nicole Way, she argued that the flawed absentee ballot report used by the Republicans as proof of fraud "wasn't the best report…but it wasn't fraudulent."[39]

* * *

In his final word to the court, Secretary of State Attorney Tom Ahearne began with undisputed facts.

"One of the things the Republicans and Democrats agree on is that a lot of counties made a lot of mistakes and a lot of mistakes resulted in a lot of illegal votes being counted in the 2004 governor's election," Ahearne said. "Some of the mistakes could be rectified," he said. "Others could not and remained part of the final count."[40]

Ahearne defended the neutrality of Elections Director Nick Handy, whom Republicans had accused of bias.

"He wasn't taking sides with one political party or another," Ahearne said. "He was taking sides with the truth, regardless of what one political party wanted or not."[41]

Ahearne argued that Handy had criticized issues that Republicans subsequently dropped, proving his evaluation of those claims correct. He strongly criticized Republicans for launching a campaign that alleged election worker errors had disenfranchised military voters.

"At a time when we have soldiers fighting and dying in Iraq and Afghanistan, the idea that a political party is going to promote an idea like that when it's outright false is, to be conservative, not responsible."[42]

Ahearne also defended Secretary Reed as a fair and impartial election administrator, who has been sued by both political parties at various times during the elections process.

"The simple and undisputable fact here is the Secretary of State has consistently advocated for development of a full and complete record regardless of what the political parties want, consistently advocated for a rational and workable interpretation of our election contest statute regardless of what the political parties wanted. He has consistently acted as the Secretary of State for all of Washington, not the Secretary of State for the Republicans or the Democrats. And frankly that's the kind of public official we want."[43]

He reminded the court that the question before it was not what any of the parties thought was fair or right.

"The question is what does our election contest statute as currently written require," he said.

* * *

Just before the court recessed, Republican Attorney Harry Korrell gave the last word.

"It would be supremely unfair to the people of the State of Washington if its largest county can have the most backward elections system and result in a cancellation of the votes of the voters in the other counties. We ask the Court to take seriously the evidence, take seriously the arguments of all the parties. But at the end of the day we ask the Court to set aside the results of this election."[44]

Nine days of televised testimony and argument challenging Washington's closest Governor's race of all time had finished.

Across the state, voters, politicos, Dino Rossi, and Christine Gregoire began a three-day wait for Judge Bridges' decision.

Endnotes

1. Tim Haeck, 2004 election coverage, KIRO 710 Newsradio, Bonneville International Corporation, May 23, 2005.
2. Dale Foreman, *Borders et al. v. King County et al.*, Vol. I E-Transcript, p. 11.
3. Ibid.
4. Ibid.
5. Kevin Hamilton, *Borders et al. v. King County et al.* Vol. 1 E-Transcript, p. 35.
6. Ibid, p. 42.
7. Jeff Even, *Borders et al. v. King County et al.*, Vol. 1 E-Transcript.
8. Dale Foreman, *Borders et al. v. King County et al.*, Vol. I E-Transcript, p. 147.
9. Evelyn Arnold, *Borders et al. v. King County et al.*, Vol. II E-Transcript, p. 277.
10. Jenny Durkan and Evelyn Arnold, *Borders et al. v. King County et al.*, Vol. II E-Transcript, p. 279.
11. David Postman, "Leadoff Witness Key for GOP?" *Seattle Times*, May 25, 2005.
12. Robert Maguire and Bill Huennekens, *Borders et al. v. King County et al.*, Vol. II—E-Transcript, p. 331.
13. Associated Press, "Election Trial: Democrats Attack GOP Data Analyst's Testimony," *Tri-City Herald*, May 26, 2005.
14. Nicole Way, *Borders et al. v. King County et al.*, Vol. III E-Transcript, pp. 663–37.
15. Ibid., p. 626.
16. David Postman. "Numbers Speak for Themselves, GOP Says." *Seattle Times*, May 26, 2005.
17. Ibid.
18. Nick Handy, "Chat with Washington Elections Director Nick Handy," *Olympian*, May 26, 2005.

19. Danny Westneat, "Shame on GOP for Trial Sham," *Seattle Times*, May 27, 2005.
20. Kevin Hamilton, *Borders et al. v. King County et al.*, Vol. V E-Transcript, p. 1008.
21. Judge John Bridges, *Borders et al. v. King County et al.*, Vol. V E-Transcript, p. 1060.
22. Dale Foreman and Nick Handy, *Border v. King County et al.*, Vol. VI E-Transcript, pp. 1253–54.
23. David Postman, "'Secretary of State's Office Is Not Neutral,' GOP Says," *Seattle Times*, June 1, 2005.
24. Ibid.
25. Ibid.
26. David Postman, "Week Two: Election Trial Dispatches, for One State Official, a Short-lived Retirement," *Seattle Times*, www.seattletimes.com, May 31, 2005.
27. David Postman, "Elections Chief Logan Put on Hot Seat—by Judge," *Seattle Times*, June 2, 2005.
28. Gregory Roberts, "Expert Says GOP's Solution for Illegal Votes 'Just Doesn't Work,'" *Post-Intelligencer*, June 2, 2005.
29. David Postman, "Week Two: Election Trial Dispatches, Dems' Statistical Expert Says Not Possible to Know If Gregoire Won," *Seattle Times*, www.seattletimes.com, June 1, 2005.
30. Ibid.
31. Ibid.
32. Rich Roesler, "Eye on Olympia, Respondents Exhibit 8093," *Spokesman Review*, www.spokesmanreview.com/blogs/olympia, June 5, 2005.
33. Harry Korrell, *Borders et al. v. King County et al.*, Vol. IX E-Transcript, p. 2121.
34. David Postman, "Election Case Is about Trust Attorneys Say," *Seattle Times*, June 4, 2005.
35. Ibid.
36. The Democrats had introduced depositions from 5 felons, 4 of whom indicated they voted for Dino Rossi and 1 who indicated he voted for Ruth Bennett.
37. Jenny Durkan, *Borders et al. v. King County et al.*, Vol. IX E-Transcript, p. 2122.
38. Gregory Roberts, "Election Case in Judge's Hands," *Post-Intelligencer*, June 4, 2005.
39. David Postman, "Week Two: Election Trial Dispatches," *Seattle Times*, June 3, 2005.
40. Ibid.
41. Ibid.
42. Tom Ahearne, *Borders et al. v. King County et al.*, Vol. IX E-Transcript, p. 2169.
43. Ibid., pp. 2171–72.
44. Harry Korrell, *Borders et al. v. King County et al.*, Vol. IX, E-Transcript, pp. 2177, 2188.

This Court is not in a position to fix the deficiencies in the election process.

Chapter Eleven

And the Governor Is…

Twists and turns that threatened to unravel the nation's closest Governor's race of all time came to a head on June 6, 2005. After a nerve-racking seven months, two people aspiring for the Governorship prepared for a verdict that could alter the course of political history.

Republican Dino Rossi waited with his family.

From their respective offices at the State Capitol, Democrat Christine Gregoire and Secretary of State Sam Reed huddled with staff to watch the live broadcast of the oral decision.

"The Court is rising as Judge Bridges is taking the bench. Let's listen in," reported KIRO Radio's Tim Haeck.[1]

"I have been asked in closing argument to send a message," Judge John Bridges told the courtroom. "I'm going to decline that invitation. This Court is not in a position to fix the deficiencies in the election process that we heard about in this courtroom over the past nine days."[2]

Before ruling on the court case in front of him, Judge Bridges addressed major problems in the elections process that had sparked controversy for months. He called on voters to demand immediate improvements from their government, beginning with the culture at King County Elections.

"Almost anyone who works in state or local government knows exactly what this culture is. It's inertia. It's selfishness. It's taking our paycheck but not doing the work. It's not caring about either our fellow workers or the public we are supposed to serve. It's not taking responsibility. It's refusing to be held accountable. And so it is the voters who should send the message."[3]

The Decision

Felon Voters

Bridges then spoke for roughly an hour, taking in turn each argument to nullify the election of Christine Gregoire. He began by considering the hotly contested felon counts turned over by each political party.

To argue their case, Republicans had presented the court with evidence of 754 illegal votes, predominately cast by felons in Gregoire-supporting precincts, whereas Democrats came forward with proof of 647 illegal votes cast by felons in Rossi strongholds. (The Democratic Party also presented facts accusing 6 mentally incompetent people of voting illegally and 19 others for voting under the names of deceased persons.)

Bridges accepted that these ballots were illegal votes, but determined in nearly all cases that the political parties came up short—failing to prove which candidate the felons selected, or even whether they voted for Governor at all. Only 4 ballots in support of Dino Rossi and 1 vote for Libertarian candidate Ruth Bennett were confirmed as illegal votes, and as such, would be subtracted from the election results for the official record.

"Bridges discounts felon-voter evidence," posted the *Seattle Times* as the judge announced his decision.[4]

Bridges further recognized that provisional ballots were mishandled by election workers, who failed to check credentials. Also, ballots had been incorrectly fed through the machines. But according to the judge, no information existed as to which candidate may have benefited from these mistakes. Bridges also stated that the voters who improperly cast their ballots should not be disenfranchised.

The court determined that as many as nine counties did not reconcile the number of people credited with voting and the number of ballots actually cast, but he called crediting a post-election procedure with no impact on the integrity of the election results. These discrepancies involved some 1,400 votes and helped bungle the accounting. Regarding King County's portion, 875 absentee ballots, Bridges said: "Very little, if any, evidence has been provided to create an inference that absentee ballots were tabulated without signature verification."[5]

Bridges also confirmed six cases of double voting.

Of the significant problems with King County's new voter registration system and the much talked about falsified ballot report produced by Nicole Way and Garth Fell, Bridges did not mince words.

"Ms. Way had expressed concerns to her superiors about the ability of the new software to properly verify the absentee ballot numbers. The problems in King County are associated with and result from a lack of communication, lack of taking responsibility for actions, a lower level of accountability, and difficulty in documenting procedures."[6]

Evidence for the provocative fraud claims alleging that "someone stuffed the ballot box" did not weigh heavily with the judge. According to Bridges, the allegations came too late with too little proof. He was not convinced misconduct of any kind changed the outcome of the election despite its record-thin margin of victory.

Bridges decided fraud could not now be claimed, since it had been neither pled nor disclosed by the Republicans. (The Republicans had disclosed their list on April 15, but did not allege any election official errors. On May 9, the Democrats submitted their list of illegal voters and election official errors.) To the extent that the Republicans had claimed it, Bridges said they had failed to meet the higher burden of clear, cogent, and convincing evidence.

"With respect to King County, there is no evidence that the significant errors which occurred resulted from intentional misconduct or someone's desire to manipulate the election. There is no evidence that anybody associated with any of the candidates in the governor's race had anything to do with causing the errors. There is no evidence that has been produced in this court to suggest that the errors resulted from partisan bias."[7]

"No testimony has been placed before the Court to suggest fraud or intentional misconduct. Election officials attempted to perform their responsibilities in a fair and impartial manner."[8]

Expert Witnesses—Proportional Deduction

The expert witnesses who declared Rossi the true winner according to the theory of proportional deduction did not persuade Bridges either. The judge did not accept the notion that a "felon" would likely vote the same as his neighbors. Bridges added that even if this theory was applied, he was not convinced Rossi would receive more legal votes than Gregoire.

"Indeed, the Court is more inclined to conclude that if this type of testimony is properly admissible, then Ms. Gregoire would have prevailed under a theory of proportional deduction."[9]

Conclusions of Law

In his conclusions of law, Bridges ruled:

- The Court had jurisdiction over the parties and the subject matter of the case.
- The Court should exercise restraint in interfering with the elective process.
- Unless an election is clearly invalid, the Court should not overturn a verdict of the people.

In its final judgment, the court accepted that 1,678 illegal votes were cast in the 2004 General Election by:

- 1,401 convicted felons.
- 19 people casting ballots belonging to deceased voters.
- 6 double voters.
- 96 people voting provisional ballots in King County, and 79 voters casting them in Pierce County.
- An additional 77 illegal votes cast in Pierce County.

Bridges referenced State law (RCW 29A.68.110), which prohibits the court from setting aside any election due to illegal votes unless it can be shown that those votes change the outcome of an election. Bridges concluded: By "clear and convincing evidence," 4 illegal felon votes were cast for Dino Rossi and 1 for Ruth Bennett.

"There is no evidence, however, in this record that Ms. Gregoire received any illegal votes. Indeed, there has been no evidence produced that Ms. Gregoire received any of the 2,820 votes claimed by petitioners in their closing argument."[10]

"The Court concludes further that no matter the number of illegal votes, whether they total 1,678, as determined by this Court, or 2,820, as argued by petitioners in their closing, this election may not be set aside merely because the number of illegal or invalid votes exceed the margin of victory, because the election contest statute requires the contestant to show that the illegal votes or misconduct changed the election result. The Washington State legislature has, by enacting RCW 29A.68.110 and 29A 68.020, removed any other choice from this Court's discretion."[11]

Finally, Judge Bridges ruled that the election of Christine Gregoire would stand.

"This Court concludes that the election contest petition should be dismissed with prejudice and the certification of Ms. Gregoire as governor confirmed."[12]

All told, *Borders et al. v. King County et al.*—the historic court case requiring millions of dollars, months of laborious work, numerous depositions, and record-setting public information requests —resulted in a net change of four votes between the two top candidates who wished to be Governor. Christine Gregoire remained the State's chief executive—only her margin of victory had widened from 129 votes to 133.

"There you have it—the ruling from Chelan County Superior Court—Judge John Bridges dismissing what the Republicans were claiming as far as the election of Governor Gregoire," reported KIRO Radio.[13]

"They have won. They have defended the election of Governor Christine Gregoire," stated KIRO's Tim Haeck.

Seconds after the ruling, elated Democratic lawyers hugged before the cameras.

"I'm personally relieved. God bless my family," said an emotional Christine Gregoire. "God bless those who in the days leading up to this sent me their prayers and wishes. I am happy for myself. I'm happy for the state of Washington that we can finally move on here."[14]

Judge Bridges had barely exited the court room when the party chairmen reached for the microphones.

"We're here. It happened. Now it's time to move on," Democrat Paul Berendt told KIRO Radio.[15]

"It's a shame Dino Rossi didn't graciously concede this election in December when all the votes were counted. Instead, he put the people of Washington through this expensive and unnecessary legal battle."[16]

But Republicans had their own take on the ruling and its impact, expressing first their obvious disappointment. "It's not the ruling we were hoping for but that's the whole point of having an election contest," said Rossi spokeswoman Mary Lane.[17]

But Lane was quick to reiterate that Republicans disagreed with the judge.

"When you have errors far in excess of the margin of victory it sets the stage or a precedence to say—well—you can't say who they voted for or if they voted for governor so we're just going to ignore the problem."[18]

State Republican Party Chairman Chris Vance went further, holding King County Executive Ron Sims accountable for the election troubles, and accusing Judge Bridges of setting what he called a "ridiculous" standard for election lawsuits.[19]

Blog writers scrambled to offer their opinions. "My worst fears about distributed vote fraud have proven true. Our current laws (and administrative practices in King County) encourage individuals to commit vote fraud—and make it extraordinarily difficult to prove their fraudulent votes changed the results of any given election," wrote John Miller on soundpolitics.com.[20]

Secretary Reed called the decision "forthright, practical and clear," and said he hoped the ruling would rebuild voter confidence.

"I think it sets the basis for restoring that trust. I would expect in the short run there will be maybe less trust because it exposed problems, illegal votes, and mistakes."[21]

"Throughout this process, my office has not advocated for either candidate. As an interested party, we support full disclosure of the facts and evidence, the correct application of Washington State election law, and the precedent this historic case will set. This razor-thin election is an opportunity to strengthen Washington elections and the democratic process," said the Secretary in a media statement.[22]

Reed did say he wished Republicans would have claimed fraud earlier and produce evidence. "I thought overall they had a good case, and a right to make it."

"What we wanted was a full trial with an airing of all the facts and a fair ruling on the merits," Reed's attorney Ahearne said, "and I think this judge delivered."[23]

No Appeal

Late that afternoon, Dino Rossi held a press conference at his Bellevue campaign headquarters to announce his next move.

"With today's decision, and because of the political makeup of the Washington State Supreme Court which makes it almost impossible to overturn this ruling, I am ending the election contest. Now I'd like to wish Christine Gregoire and her family all the best over the next three and a half years," said the Republican.[24]

As he ended one of the longest bids for Governor in history, Rossi took no questions from reporters.

Chief Justice Gerry Alexander of the Washington State Supreme Court later said that he was "reluctant to get into something with Mr. Rossi" over the latter's critical comments regarding the State Supreme Court. Alexander said there was no basis for Rossi's assertion.

"I've been on the court for ten years and the court simply does not have a partisan bias. In the ten years I've been here, I don't think the court has ever said anything or written anything that could lead someone to that conclusion."[25]

After the press conference, a KIRO reporter described Rossi's take on the seven-month ordeal.

"He believes that shining the light on various problems in our election system was the right thing to do. He stands by his decision to go through this long legal process."[26]

Rossi's decision and the court ruling dominated virtually every news media outlet in the state, and attracted attention across the country.

> **"Judge Upholds Washington Governor's Election"** noted *USA Today*.[27]
>
> **"Judge Dismisses Lawsuit over Washington Election"** reported the *New York Times*.[28]

The media did not let up, as indicated in a blunt *Seattle Times* editorial by Joni Balter. "Dino Rossi and the Republicans were shellacked in the Court of Chelan County. Point by point, the judge rejected their inferences and wild conjecture in the effort to overturn the closest governor's race in state history…

"Rossi remained dignified throughout, with the notable exception of his graceless swipe at the State Supreme Court. Rossi said he would not take the election contest to the state's highest court because the political makeup of the Supreme Court would have made it almost impossible to get the decision overturned. That is ten tons of hooey."[29]

The political knocks kept coming.

All Over but the Pouting

The public, of course, responded with views all across the board, as seen in letters to the *Seattle Times* editor.

Vicky Monk of Renton wrote, "Thank you, Judge John Bridges, for being a voice of reason during these troubled times.

"My message to the Republican Party: You are doing far more harm than good when you challenge elections across the country that don't go your way. These are the actions of whiners, pouting brats, and poor losers.

"What has happened to integrity, to shaking your opponent's hand, to acting like gentlemen (and women)? You set a bad example for our younger generation who are learning from your extremely poor behavior.

"Change your strategy before you irreparably harm your party."[30]

Disparity's Over

Joe O'Donnell from Kirkland observed, "Judge John Bridges ruled that there were 1,678 illegal votes, then ordered them to be subtracted from the official total number of votes in the state. So if you add Libertarian Ruth Bennett's,

Dino Rossi's, and Christine Gregoire's total official votes, they add up to more than the total votes cast.

"More votes for the candidates than voters...A fitting end to the 2004 election."[31]

The Judge Favors the Status Quo over the Evidence

Chuck Penk of Renton exclaimed, "Of course there were illegal votes. People have been charged with it.

"Of course there were errors. The Democrats admitted it.

"Of course there was fraud. How else do you explain votes being found week after week and month after month?

"This is a sad day for democracy in America. Sixteen-hundred illegal votes in a race won by 129 votes! And the judge doesn't think that is wrong. He had an excellent chance to send a message. Instead, nothing has to change and nothing will change.

"The Democrats of King County have now proven they can put whoever they want into the governor's office."[32]

* * *

A few days later, the bulk of the commentary on the Gregoire-Rossi contest finally came to an end. With a touch of humor, reporter Peter Callaghan of Tacoma's *News Tribune* was almost sorry to see the story conclude:

"What do you mean it's over?

"The election that wouldn't end has ended? It was supposed to last at least another month or two, long enough for teams of lawyers to prepare reams of legal briefs for a final showdown before the nine robed oracles at the Temple of Justice.

"It was supposed to last long enough for another few dozen stories, another handful of columns, another sack full of TV soundbites, another million words on talk radio, another billion bits in the blogosphere."[33]

The Gregoire-Rossi race ended the way it began when the unlikely Republican challenger closed in on the well-known three-term Attorney General—in the harsh glare of the media spotlight.

However, veteran candidates and political junkies agreed that June 6, 2005, simply marked the end of one historic race. New, popular candidates were sure to emerge, and many voters would again leap across Washington's political divide. Politics would go on.

"Well, politics is never going to end. What would you do for a living if politics ended? I get paid to run campaigns to elect Republicans, that's what the Republican party does, there's nothing unusual about that. Paul Berendt does the same, if we went away what would you do? You'd be bored to death," said Chris Vance of the Washington State Republican Party.[34]

Endnotes

1. Tim Haeck, 2004 election coverage, KIRO 710 Newsradio, Bonneville International Corporation, June 6, 2005.
2. Judge John Bridges, *Borders et al. v. King County et al.*, oral decision, Chelan County Superior Court, June 6, 2005.
3. Ibid.
4. David Postman, www.seattletimes.nwsource.com, June 6, 2005.
5. Judge John Bridges, *Borders et al. v. King County et al.*, oral decision, Chelan County Superior Court, June 6, 2005.
6. Ibid.
7. Ibid.
8. Ibid.
9. Ibid.
10. Ibid.
11. Ibid.
12. Ibid.
13. Tim Haeck, 2004 election coverage, KIRO 710 Newsradio, Bonneville International Corporation, June 6, 2005.
14. David Postman, "Rossi Will Not Appeal Election Ruling," *Seattle Times*, June 6, 2005.
15. 2004 election coverage, KIRO 710 Newsradio, Bonneville International Corporation, June 6, 2005.
16. KING Television, Belo Corporation, www.king5.com.
17. 2004 election coverage, KIRO 710 Newsradio, Bonneville International Corporation, June 6, 2005.
18. Ibid.
19. David Postman and Ralph Thomas, "After Election-contest Ruling: It's all Over but the Sniping, *Seattle Times*, June 8, 2005.
20. John Miller, "Sound Politics: First Thoughts on Judge Bridges' Decision," www.soundpolitics.com, June 6, 2005.
21. David Postman, "Rossi Will Not Appeal Election Ruling" *Seattle Times*, June 6, 2005.
22. Office of the Secretary of State, "Reed's Statement on Judge John Bridge's Ruling in the Election Contest," media statement," June 6, 2005.
23. Gregory Roberts, "Judge Upholds Gregoire's Election; Rossi Won't Appeal," *Post-Intelligencer*, June 6, 2005.
24. Gordy Holt and Chris McGann, "Rossi Ends the Fight, Judge Upholds Gregoire's Election Victory." *Post-Intelligencer*, June 7, 2005.
25. David Postman and Ralph Thomas, "After Election-contest Ruling, It's all Over but the Sniping," *Seattle Times*, June 8, 2005.
26. 2004 election coverage, KIRO 710 News radio, Bonneville International Corporation, June 6, 2005.
27. *USA Today*, June 6, 2005.
28. Eli Sanders, *New York Times*, June 7, 2005.
29. Joni Balter, "Rossi's in Great Position to be the GOP's Next...?" *Seattle Times*, June 9, 2005.
30. Vicky Monk to the *Seattle Times* editor, "All Over but the Pouting," *Seattle Times*, June 7, 2005.
31. Joe O'Donnell to the *Seattle Times* editor, "Disparity's Over," *Seattle Times*, June 7, 2005.
32. Chuck Penk to the *Seattle Times* editor, "The Judge Favors the Status Quo over the Evidence," *Seattle Times*, June 7, 2005.
33. Peter Callaghan, "Help Us, Dino—Tell Us What's Left to Write About," *News Tribune*, June 9, 2005.
34. Robert Mak and Mike Cate, "Trial and Error," KING Television, Belo Corporation, June 15, 2005.

Epilogue

Over the next several years, the closest governor's race in American history reverberated across the state—spurring further debate, and serving as a catalyst for improving elections policy like never before. No other contest in modern state history had polarized voters in such a way, or commanded as much attention and energy.

Sam Reed, still at the helm of the Office of the Secretary of State, faced an immediate and monumental challenge—the voting process, designed to preserve and protect First Amendment rights, was deemed broken by the very people it was intended to serve. Well into 2006, critics continued to mock Washington elections with jokes about "dead people voting" or with emotional claims of a "stolen election."

Aided by county auditors, task forces, legislators, and voters, Reed led the charge for secure and accurate elections. This collaborative effort resulted in some 1,280 changes to the voting process in a dramatic overhaul. Among the most significant were extensive changes to voter registration, and adopting an earlier date for the State Primary, allowing more turnaround time between the primary and general elections to better serve overseas and military voters.

The struggle between the political parties and Reed over the style of the State's Primary continued, eventually going to the U.S. Supreme Court on appeal. State Attorney General Rob McKenna, representing Reed, personally argued and won the case. But despite the ruling of the court, the parties continued to lodge complaints against the State's Primary system.

* * *

The disputed gubernatorial election also was blamed as a factor in the firing of U.S. Attorney John McKay, who served the Western District of Washington.

After a Department of Justice investigation, a top DOJ official informed McKay: "The Administration wants to go in a different direction, and they would like you to resign." Media reports linked McKay's sudden dismissal to the fact that he did not step into the alleged voter fraud issue in the Governor's race.

"Had anyone at the Justice Department or the [Bush] White House ordered me to pursue any matter criminally in the 2004 governor's election, I would have resigned," McKay told the *Seattle Times*. "There was no evidence, and I am not going to drag innocent people in front of a grand jury."[1]

On January 26, 2007, John McKay stepped down.

* * *

As 2008 approached, the embattled key participants of the 2004 election pondered whether to run again for public office.

Despite his reputation as a national elections expert and his popularity with Washington voters, Sam Reed prepared for a tough campaign. Politically, Reed said he was a "marked man" and considered a "traitor" by some former Republican allies. According to the Secretary, a friendly, astute Republican leader told a Reed confidante: "There's no way Sam Reed is going to get reelected in 2008." Some still criticized Reed for certifying the election, despite the fact that he would have violated his oath of office by not doing so.

Meanwhile, fellow Republican Dino Rossi appeared to be grooming for a second run for Governor. He released a self-published autobiography, *Dino Rossi: Lessons in Leadership, Business, Politics and Life*, created a policy foundation, and maintained a profile on the public stage.

"He's everywhere. He's speaking a lot. He hasn't gotten bogged down in specific issues. He's stayed above it," said Republican political consultant Brett Bader.[2]

The decision to take on another grueling campaign was not lightly made, especially for a family man like Rossi. But on October 25, 2007, Rossi publicly announced his candidacy with a promise to balance the budget and bring much-needed change to the State.

"Nothing will change in Olympia if we keep the same old crowd in charge," Rossi said. "They have had their turn."[3]

"All we have to do is ask ourselves, are we better off today as a state than we were three years ago," countered Gregoire in the media. "You bet we are. I'm not willing to go back to the old days."[4]

Gregoire, in declaring her candidacy, touted success in education and the creation of a rainy day fund for State government.

In August, the top-two Primary predictably put both contenders on the November ballot, officially launching a fierce rematch between Gregoire and Rossi.

The likelihood that history would be repeated in another staggering election dispute seemed inconceivable, but it could not be dismissed. The polls again locked the two candidates in a statistical dead heat.

Their campaigns and those of the major political parties moved on at an exhaustive pace, airing a relentless series of attack ads. Democrats attempted to link Rossi to an unpopular Republican president, while Republicans accused Gregoire's administration of losing track of sex predators.

Both candidates, however, recognized the impact of the continuous onslaught of negative ads.

"This is demeaning to the office we both seek," said Rossi.[5]

"I am chagrined at these negative ads, multimillion-dollar dishonest negative attacks," said Gregoire during the candidates' last televised debate.[6]

In the November 2008 General Election, the 133-vote difference in 2004 between Rossi and Gregoire had widened into a 7 point lead and a comfortable 200,000 vote margin for Gregoire. This time, no significant election problems were reported.

Dino Rossi told his supporters: "I am extremely proud of the campaign we have run, and together we accomplished a lot. This campaign was a citizens' movement with over 55,500 contributors—more than any other race in Washington state history. We brought new people into politics, who had never been involved before, and got people excited about improving our state."[7]

Gregoire, whose fate after election day in 2004 had hinged on a court decision coming months later, declared victory within hours of the polls closing in 2008.

"Tonight the voters in Washington sent a message that they want a governor who shares their values of providing children healthcare, protecting the environment, and creating jobs," said Gregoire in a press release.[8]

Sam Reed decisively won a third term after a three-year-long exhaustive effort to advance elections and undo the public's negative perceptions of Washington's voting process.

As in 2004, the 2008 elections made history. Barack Obama, the nation's first African-American president, carried the day in a record turnout. In Washington State, a record-setting 84.61 percent of eligible voters cast ballots.

"I couldn't be prouder of Washington voters for taking part in this crucial election in such dramatic fashion," said Reed. "This has been an amazing year for our country and our state."[9]

As it turned out, the longest election of 2008 occurred in Minnesota, where Al Franken challenged incumbent Norm Coleman for a U.S. Senate seat. Former Washington Democratic Party Chair Paul Berendt flew to the Midwest to assist Franken.

"There were some people at the national party who put the call in to us and asked us to get people with experience back there," said Berendt. "I wanted to be helpful. I wanted every ballot to count. I felt it was worth my while to be going."[10]

A mere 225 votes finally allowed Franken, the Democrat, to capture the office. The Minnesota election demonstrated, yet again, the power of a single voice in a democracy.

* * *

For the Office of the Secretary of State, the 2004 Governor's election will long illustrate the strength of the voting process. Though far from perfect at the time, the historic contest provided a fair, even-handed forum for both candidates to have their day in court, and later led to unprecedented reforms in the elections processes in the State of Washington.

Voters, however, may remain divided over the legacy of the 2004 Governor's Election and whether it illuminates the failings of a system and those in charge, or will stand as modern history's bona fide example of a working democracy. As Gonzaga University articulated in bestowing the Gonzaga Law Medal, this was the Secretary of State's finest hour.

"Secretary Reed's integrity and actions in respect of the rule of law merit this recognition and have impelled the School of Law, its faculty, and administration to stand up, applaud, and bestow on him its highest honor."[11]

Endnotes

1. David Bowermaster, "McKay 'Stunned' by Report on Bush," *Seattle Times*, March 13, 2007.
2. Neil Modie, "Will Dino Rossi Run Again for Governor? Even He Doesn't Know," *Post-Intelligencer*, March 12, 2007.
3. Ralph Thomas, "Rossi Announces Bid for Governor," *Seattle Times*, October 25, 2007.
4. Ibid.
5. David Horsey, "Gregoire and Rossi: Minor Leaguers," blog.seattlepi.nwsource.com/davidhorsey/archives/151618.asp, October 15, 2008.
6. Jim Brunner, "Final Face-off: Rossi, Gregoire Debate Who's Best Leader, Who Gets Blame," *Seattle Times*, October 15, 2008.
7. Dino Rossi for Governor, "Rossi Statement on Election Results," November 6, 2008.
8. Chris Gregoire for Governor, "Gov. Gregoire Claims Victory," November 5, 2008.
9. Office of the Secretary of State, "Washington's Voter Turnout Breaks Record," press release, November 25, 2008.
10. Brad Shannon, "Minnesota Recount Stirs Memories of Gregoire-Rossi 'messiness,'" *Olympian*, December 17, 2008.
11. Gonzaga Law Medal, bestowed by the Gonzaga Law School, May 10, 2005.

Appendices

Appendix 1

THE MACHINE AND MANUAL RECOUNTS

Christine Gregoire (D)

COUNTY	Initial Results	Machine Recount	Manual Recount	Gain/Loss
Adams	1,517	1,529	1,529	**0**
Asotin	3,524	3,525	3,530	**5**
Benton	19,830	19,831	19,834	**3**
Chelan	10,074	10,077	10,077	**0**
Clallam	16,225	16,226	16,230	**4**
Clark	72,797	72,800	72,828	**28**
Columbia	670	671	671	**0**
Cowlitz	20,236	20,207	20,204	**-3**
Douglas	4,357	4,359	4,360	**1**
Ferry	1,275	1,278	1,278	**0**
Franklin	4,968	4,967	4,977	**10**
Garfield	427	428	428	**0**
Grant	7,800	7,826	7,821	**-5**
Garys Habor	13,713	13,719	13,729	**10**
Island	16,888	16,888	16,895	**7**
Jefferson	10,641	10,642	10,650	**8**
King	505,243	505,836	506,194	**358**
Kitsap	56,149	56,164	56,236	**72**
Kittitas	6,106	6,125	6,125	**0**
Klickitat	3,919	3,919	3,919	**0**
Lewis	10,243	10,245	10,247	**2**
Lincoln	1,850	1,850	1,850	**0**
Mason	11,787	11,788	11,797	**9**
Okanogan	6,100	6,101	6,107	**6**
Pacific	5,209	5,210	5,210	**0**
Pend Oreille	2,561	2,567	2,567	**0**
Pierce	144,957	145,199	145,431	**232**
San Juan	5,872	5,872	5,872	**0**
Skagit	23,195	23,266	23,250	**-16**
Skamania	2,232	2,232	2,233	**1**
Snohomish	138,939	139,070	139,189	**119**
Spokane	90,452	90,573	90,581	**8**
Stevens	6,992	6,992	6,992	**0**
Thurston	58,953	58,955	58,970	**15**
Wahkiakum	993	993	993	**0**
Walla Walla	7,947	8,006	8,008	**2**
Whatcom	44,053	44,056	44,072	**16**
Whitman	7,724	7,715	7,722	**7**
Yakima	24,735	24,735	24,755	**20**
Total	1,371,153	1,372,442	1,373,361	**919**
	48.8666%	48.8702%	48.8730%	**0.0028%**

Final Results

The vote totals opposite are the final and official results. In June 2005, Chelan County Superior Court Judge John Bridges issued a ruling changing the final vote totals.

Dino Rossi (R)

COUNTY	Initial Results	Machine Recount	Manual Recount	Gain/Loss
Adams	3,459	3,486	3,481	**-5**
Asotin	4,905	4,904	4,914	**10**
Benton	44,888	44,890	44,895	**5**
Chelan	18,436	18,437	18,438	**1**
Clallam	18,831	18,832	18,836	**4**
Clark	85,887	85,894	85,924	**30**
Columbia	1,370	1,370	1,371	**1**
Cowlitz	20,087	20,047	20,045	**-2**
Douglas	8,662	8,666	8,667	**1**
Ferry	1,898	1,900	1,900	**0**
Franklin	10,618	10,619	10,634	**15**
Garfield	839	840	840	**0**
Grant	17,385	17,429	17,431	**2**
Garys Habor	13,444	13,449	13,457	**8**
Island	19,992	19,997	20,000	**3**
Jefferson	7,293	7,289	7,295	**6**
King	350,779	351,127	351,306	**179**
Kitsap	57,712	57,693	57,775	**82**
Kittitas	9,541	9,567	9,567	**0**
Klickitat	4,766	4,767	4,767	**0**
Lewis	20,838	20,842	20,851	**9**
Lincoln	3,685	3,686	3,686	**0**
Mason	12,505	12,507	12,519	**12**
Okanogan	9,451	9,450	9,460	**10**
Pacific	4,730	4,730	4,730	**0**
Pend Oreille	3,364	3,366	3,368	**2**
Pierce	157,443	157,704	157,905	**201**
San Juan	3,661	3,660	3,660	**0**
Skagit	27,135	27,224	27,219	**-5**
Skamania	2,522	2,522	2,525	**3**
Snohomish	145,423	145,553	145,628	**75**
Spokane	105,435	105,569	105,584	**15**
Stevens	12,293	12,293	12,295	**2**
Thurston	49,409	49,413	49,426	**13**
Wahkiakum	1,099	1,100	1,099	**-1**
Walla Walla	14,240	14,277	14,290	**13**
Whatcom	41,978	41,978	42,000	**22**
Whitman	9,367	9,363	9,365	**2**
Yakima	46,044	46,044	46,079	**35**
Total	1,371,414	1,372,484	1,373,232	**748**
	48.8759%	48.8717%	48.8685%	**-0.00320%**

Christine Gregoire (D)	1,373,361	48.8731%
Dino Rossi (R)	1,373,228	48.8684%
Ruth Bennett (L)	63,464	2.2585%
Total	2,810,054	100.0000%

Ruth Bennett (L)

COUNTY	Initial Results	Machine Recount	Manual Recount	Gain/Loss
Adams	79	81	81	**0**
Asotin	193	193	193	**0**
Benton	1,119	1,118	1,118	**0**
Chelan	523	523	523	**0**
Clallam	919	919	920	**1**
Clark	4,123	4,123	4,123	**0**
Columbia	37	37	37	**0**
Cowlitz	1,094	1,093	1,094	**1**
Douglas	218	219	219	**0**
Ferry	118	118	118	**0**
Franklin	226	227	227	**0**
Garfield	25	25	25	**0**
Grant	534	535	535	**0**
Garys Habor	575	575	575	**0**
Island	814	814	814	**0**
Jefferson	465	466	466	**0**
King	18,906	18,936	18,952	**16**
Kitsap	3,097	3,090	3,097	**7**
Kittitas	275	277	277	**0**
Klickitat	265	265	265	**0**
Lewis	756	756	757	**1**
Lincoln	100	100	100	**0**
Mason	681	682	680	**-2**
Okanogan	465	465	468	**3**
Pacific	295	295	296	**1**
Pend Oreille	179	179	179	**0**
Pierce	7,230	7,241	7,255	**14**
San Juan	320	321	320	-1
Skagit	1,260	1,267	1,264	**-3**
Skamania	178	178	178	**0**
Snohomish	6,842	6,852	6,861	**9**
Spokane	3,872	3,878	3,881	**3**
Stevens	566	566	566	**0**
Thurston	2,574	2,575	2,575	**0**
Wahkiakum	61	61	61	**0**
Walla Walla	376	381	378	**-3**
Whatcom	2,177	2,177	2,179	2
Whitman	458	457	457	**0**
Yakima	1,351	1,351	1,351	**0**
Total	63,346	63,416	63,465	**49**
	2.2576%	2.2581%	2.2585%	**0.004%**

Appendix 2

FROM GROUND ZERO OF THE ROSSI-GREGOIRE DRAMA TO WINNING ELECTION REFORM

A Look Inside King County since 2004

Shortly after the election and the recounts, King County began transforming its voting process to rebuild public trust and confidence. The county:

- Established new procedures to reconcile and account for all mail ballots. In August 2006, the county was recognized nationally for implementing these new procedures using the same standards as Fortune 500 companies, including Motorola, Bank of America, and General Electric.
- Implemented a poll worker training academy. The academy trained some 4,000 poll workers on security, ballot handling, and reconciliation procedures.
- Redesigned ballots so only properly registered poll voters can insert them into equipment.
- Hired private sector professionals and required employee testing and training for all permanent and temporary staff.
- Required organizational effectiveness training of all managers, supervisors, and leads—to plan for elections six months to one year in advance.
- Employed professional coaching and new project management tools to improve the culture of King County Elections. The coaching focused on accountability, meeting critical deadlines, and maintaining quality control.
- Scrubbed voter rolls daily for duplicates, deceased voters, and felons.
- Launched an online website tool that allowed voters to confirm their registrations, find their polling places, and view their personalized sample ballots.
- Established new security protocols and testing for all election equipment.
- Began testing mail ballot tabulation equipment twice each day before and after ballots were counted.

Appendix 3

NATIONAL ELECTION SUMMIT

Are America's Elections Broken?

More than two years after Washington's historic gubernatorial election, the country's leading voting experts discussed issues central to the Rossi-Gregoire contest. At a nationwide summit in March 2007, leaders and advocates remained divided over the most profound question of all: Is America's election system broken?

Many agreed that America's voting had been strengthened since Florida's contested Presidential election in 2000, but the U.S. Congress did not pass the resulting election reform package until 2002.

"There is no tolerance for the time it takes to get things right," said Election Assistance Commissioner Gracia Hillman.

Political scientist and author Thomas Mann acknowledged that the nation is more polarized today; whereas Republicans believe fraud continues, Democrats insist there are accessibility problems keeping citizens who should be voting out of the elections process. Also, because there are more close races, Mann claimed the elections themselves are under far greater scrutiny.

"Change will have to come through the broader political environment," Mann cautioned, and not just through a reform of election laws or systems. Mann warned against using public confidence as a standard for judging elections, rather the successes and failures of democracy in the closeness of the elections should depend on the way they are resolved and the partisanship of the respondents.

According to *Election Administration Reports* (April 2, 2007, edition, p. 4), Mann pointed out: "Republicans were much more confident in the election process than were Democrats following the 2000 presidential election, whereas Democrats in Washington State expressed more confidence than Republicans following the 2004 gubernatorial election."

Meanwhile, Professor Rick Hasen of the Loyola Law School outlined three standards for measuring elections: (1) a complete meltdown in which everything goes wrong and public trust suffers; (2) public confidence as manifested in opinion surveys; and (3) the competence of election administrators.

Hasen claimed election-related litigation has increased—from nearly 100 cases annually one decade ago, to roughly 250 cases per year from 2001 through 2004.

Others, such as Indiana Secretary of State Todd Rokita, were adamant that the election system is not broken, and as long as the process involves human beings, perfection will be impossible to achieve.

The summit was part of an American Enterprise Institute and Brookings Institution project, including election officials, academic experts, legal specialists, advocates for election system reform, and members of Congress.

Appendix 4
BIOGRAPHIES

Thomas Ahearne
Thomas Ahearne represented Secretary of State Sam Reed during the Republican effort to overturn the Governor's election in court. Ahearne also represented Reed in multiple cases filed after the 2004 General Election and during the subsequent recounts. Ahearne's area of expertise included constitutional law cases, election disputes, ballot title challenges, and litigation over the enforcement or validity of statutes and initiatives.

Paul Berendt
Paul Berendt served as Chairman of the Washington State Democratic Party during the 2004 elections. At the time of Berendt's subsequent resignation, he was the longest-serving State Democratic Party Chairman in the nation. During Berendt's tenure, Washington became the only state in U.S. history to elect women candidates to three top offices—two in the U.S. Senate and one as Governor.

Mark Braden
Mark Braden represented the Republican Party and gubernatorial candidate Dino Rossi. Braden was an expert on election law and governmental affairs. Braden worked as chief counsel to the Republican National Committee for 10 years prior to joining the Washington, D.C., law firm Baker Hostetler. Braden has served as the principal lawyer in many significant recounts throughout the nation in recent years.

John Bridges
Chelan County Superior Court Judge John E. Bridges presided over the legal challenge of the 2004 Governor's Election, *Borders et al. v. King County et al.* Bridges received the 2005 William Nevins Award from the Washington Judges Foundation for his work on the court challenge. *Borders et al. v. King County et al.* was filed in Chelan County Superior Court on January 7, 2005, and the case ended with Bridges' ruling on June 6, 2005. The ruling was not appealed.

Joanie Deutsch
As Communications Manager in November 2004, Joanie Deutsch assisted with all aspects of media relations, including messaging and the dissemination of information to journalists. Deutsch continued in this capacity through the recounts and resulting court case. In September 2005, Deutsch was promoted to Acting Communications Director and led all aspects of public affairs for the Office of the Secretary of State. Currently, she holds a position with the agency's

Elections Division as a policy analyst. Deutsch is a graduate of St. Martin's University in Olympia, with a degree in Political Science.

Jenny Durkan

Jenny A. Durkan served as trial counsel to defend the election of Christine Gregoire. Durkan's expertise included white collar crime and business litigation. Durkan co-chaired the bi-partisan U.S. District Judge selection committee for the Western District of Washington, and served as Executive Counsel to former Washington State Governor Mike Lowry. Durkan served on the Washington State Bar Association Board of Governors. She was appointed U.S. Attorney for Western Washington in 2009.

Jeff Even

Jeffrey T. Even, Deputy Solicitor General, served as general counsel to Secretary of State Sam Reed. Even was a widely-recognized expert on State election law. He advised Reed on most legal issues and provided additional legal services through the Solicitor General's Division of the Attorney General's Office. His work related to the contested election was recognized by an "Outstanding Employee" award from the Attorney General.

Steve Excell

Steve Excell served as Assistant Secretary of State and as Sam Reed's Chief of Staff during the 2004 elections. Excell had been appointed Chief of Staff to Washington Governor John Spellman, the last Republican Governor of the state up to the present. In addition, Excell served as U.S. Representative Joel Pritchard's Legislative Director. In the private sector, Excell was involved in all aspects of the communications business.

Dale Foreman

Dale Foreman represented Dino Rossi and the Republican Party during the court case, *Borders et al. v. King County et al.* Foreman, a former State lawmaker and candidate for Governor, was also at one time Chairman of the Washington State Republican Party.

Kevin Hamilton

Kevin Hamilton represented the Democratic Party in defending Christine Gregoire's election. Hamilton was a partner at the Seattle law firm Perkins Coie LLP. He specialized in labor and employment, litigation, constitutional law, campaign finance, and election law. Hamilton represented senators Patty Murray and Maria Cantwell, as well as the 1996 Brian Baird for Congress Campaign and the Clinton/Gore Campaign in 1996.

Nick Handy

Nick Handy, an attorney, assumed his duties as Washington State Director of Elections just six months before the 2004 General Election. Although Handy had considerable senior management involvement in state and local government, he brought no elections expertise to the job. He was hired because of his experience in public management, communications, and high profile political issues.

Trova Heffernan

Trova K. Heffernan is Director of The Legacy Project and Creative Director of the Washington State Heritage Center. From 2001 to 2008, Heffernan served as Communications Director for Washington Secretary of State Sam Reed. In addition to the 2004 gubernatorial election, Heffernan oversaw the State Primary dispute that eventually reached the U.S. Supreme Court. Trova has a journalism background in television news, having earned a B.A. in Communication from the Edward R. Murrow College of Communication at Washington State University. Until 2000, Trova worked in television news as a reporter and anchor. In 2000, she transitioned to politics as a press secretary on a gubernatorial campaign.

Harry Korrell

Harry J.F. Korrell represented the Rossi Campaign and the Republican Party as lead counsel in the 2004 gubernatorial election contest. Korrell was a partner at Davis Wright Tremaine LLP. Korrell also served as Special Assistant Attorney General representing the Washington Secretary of State in a mandamus action filed by the Governor to keep a referendum measure off the ballot. Korrell's areas of expertise are in employment and commercial litigation, including labor relations, discrimination, unfair competition, and civil rights litigation and election law.

Dean Logan

Dean Logan was in charge of King County Elections during the 2004 legal challenges. In 2003, King County Executive Ron Sims named him Director of Records, Elections, and Licensing Services. Previously, Logan served as Director of Elections for the State of Washington under Secretary Sam Reed. He began his career in Kitsap County and served there as Assistant Supervisor of Elections, Supervisor of Elections, and Chief Deputy Auditor. In 1998, Logan was appointed Kitsap County Clerk; county voters subsequently elected him to the office.

Robert Maguire

Robert J. Maguire represented the Rossi Campaign and the Republican Party in the 2004 election challenge. Maguire, a litigator, was a partner at Davis Wright Tremaine LLP. Maguire had experience representing businesses and individuals in state and federal court litigation involving fiduciary, contractual, and other commercial disputes. He tried numerous cases involving issues of trade secrets, breach of confidentiality agreements, commercial breaches of contracts, estoppel, the Uniform Commercial Code, breach of fiduciary duties, agency disputes, election disputes, real property disputes, trespass, nuisance, and easements.

John Pearson
Most notable among the seasoned Elections Division staff was Deputy Elections Director John Pearson. A 30-year veteran of the division, Pearson was widely regarded as one of the State's most knowledgeable election administrators. During the legal challenges to Gregoire's election, Pearson provided guidance in the Office of the Secretary of State and responded to the media.

Sam Reed
Washington Secretary of State Sam Reed was a defendant in multiple court cases following the 2004 election for Washington Governor. First elected to the office in November 2000, Reed won second and third terms as Secretary of State in 2004 and 2008. Reed is considered one of the nation's most accomplished Secretaries of State in the field of elections, and one of Washington State's most seasoned Secretaries ever. Secretary Reed served as President of the National Association of Secretaries of State from August 2005 to July 2006.

Ron Sims
King County Executive Ron Sims ran for Governor in the 2004 Primary but lost the Democratic nomination to Christine Gregoire. As the Chief Executive of Washington's most populous county, the longtime public servant was ultimately accountable to the voters for King County elections. Sims was first elected to the King County Council in 1985, and became Chief Executive in 1996. He was appointed Deputy Secretary of Labor by President Obama in 2009.

Russell Speidel
Russell Speidel served as co-counsel for the Washington State Democratic Party in the defense of the 2004 Governor's Election. The court case challenging Gregoire's election was Speidel's third election case. In 1987, he successfully obtained a court-ordered recall election of then Sheriff Joe Collins, who had double billed the FBI and Chelan County for the same expenses. In 1999–2000, Speidel represented without fee two local Methodist ministers, Sandy Brown and Kel Groseclose, in successfully voiding the Wenatchee mayoral selection of Gary Schoessler, who had not resided in Wenatchee for one year prior to his election.

Chris Vance
Chris Vance was the Chairman of the Washington State Republican Party during the 2004 elections. Elected chairman in 2002, Vance helped elect notable Republican candidates, including Rob McKenna, the first Republican Attorney General in more than a dozen years. Vance began his political career working for Congressman Rod Chandler. He served in the State House of Representatives from 1991 to 1993, and represented the 13th District of the King County Council from 1994 to 2001.

Index